PSYCHOLOGY
OF INTELLIGENCE ANALYSIS

PSYCHOLOGY OF INTELLIGENCE ANALYSIS

RICHARD J. HEUER, JR.

Novinka Books
New York

Library of Congress Cataloging-in-Publication Data:
Available Upon Request

ISBN: 1-59454-679-7

Published by Nova Science Publishers, Inc. ✣ New York

CONTENTS

FOREWORD[*]

Douglas MacEachin[*]

My first exposure to Dick Heuer's work was about 18 years ago, and I have never forgotten the strong impression it made on me then. That was at about the midpoint in my own career as an intelligence analyst. After another decade and a half of experience, and the opportunity during the last few years to study many historical cases with the benefit of archival materials from the former USSR and Warsaw Pact regimes, reading Heuer's latest presentation has had even more resonance.

I know from first-hand encounters that many CIA officers tend to react skeptically to treatises on analytic epistemology. This is understandable. Too often, such treatises end up prescribing models as answers to the problem. These models seem to have little practical value to intelligence analysis, which takes place not in a seminar but rather in a fast-breaking world of policy. But that is not the main problem Heuer is addressing.

What Heuer examines so clearly and effectively is how the human thought process builds its own models through which we process information. This is not a phenomenon unique to intelligence; as Heuer's research demonstrates, it is part of the natural functioning of the human cognitive process, and it has been demonstrated across a broad range of fields ranging from medicine to stock market analysis.

---

[*] Excerpted from http://www.cia.gov/csi/books/19104/index.html
[*] Douglas MacEachin is a former CIA Deputy Director of Intelligence. After 32 years with the Agency, he retired in 1997 and became a Senior Fellow at Harvard University's John F. Kennedy School of Government.

The process of analysis itself reinforces this natural function of the human brain. Analysis usually involves creating models, even though they may not be labeled as such. We set forth certain understandings and expectations about cause-and-effect relationships and then process and interpret information through these models or filters.

The discussion in Chapter 5 on the limits to the value of additional information deserves special attention, in my view--particularly for an intelligence organization. What it illustrates is that too often, newly acquired information is evaluated and processed through the existing analytic model, rather than being used to reassess the premises of the model itself. The detrimental effects of this natural human tendency stem from the raison d'etre of an organization created to acquire special, critical information available only through covert means, and to produce analysis integrating this special information with the total knowledge base.

I doubt that any veteran intelligence officer will be able to read this book without recalling cases in which the mental processes described by Heuer have had an adverse impact on the quality of analysis. How many times have we encountered situations in which completely plausible premises, based on solid expertise, have been used to construct a logically valid forecast--with virtually unanimous agreement--that turned out to be dead wrong? In how many of these instances have we determined, with hindsight, that the problem was not in the logic but in the fact that one of the premises--however plausible it seemed at the time--was incorrect? In how many of these instances have we been forced to admit that the erroneous premise was not empirically based but rather a conclusion developed from its own model (sometimes called an assumption)? And in how many cases was it determined after the fact that information had been available which should have provided a basis for questioning one or more premises, and that a change of the relevant premise(s) would have changed the analytic model and pointed to a different outcome?

The commonly prescribed remedy for shortcomings in intelligence analysis and estimates--most vociferously after intelligence "failures"--is a major increase in expertise. Heuer's research and the studies he cites pose a serious challenge to that conventional wisdom. The data show that expertise itself is no protection from the common analytic pitfalls that are endemic to the human thought process. This point has been demonstrated in many fields beside intelligence analysis.

A review of notorious intelligence failures demonstrates that the analytic traps caught the experts as much as anybody. Indeed, the data show that when experts fall victim to these traps, the effects can be aggravated by the confidence that attaches to expertise--both in their own view and in the perception of others.

These observations should in no way be construed as a denigration of the value of expertise. On the contrary, my own 30-plus years in the business of intelligence analysis biased me in favor of the view that, endless warnings of information overload notwithstanding, there is no such thing as too much information or expertise. And my own observations of CIA analysts sitting at the same table with publicly renowned experts have given me great confidence that attacks on the expertise issue are grossly misplaced. The main difference is that one group gets to promote its reputations in journals, while the other works in a closed environment in which the main readers are members of the intelligence world's most challenging audience--the policymaking community.

The message that comes through in Heuer's presentation is that information and expertise are a necessary but not sufficient means of making intelligence analysis the special product that it needs to be. A comparable effort has to be devoted to the science of analysis. This effort has to start with a clear understanding of the inherent strengths and weaknesses of the primary analytic mechanism--the human mind--and the way it processes information.

I believe there is a significant cultural element in how intelligence analysts define themselves: Are we substantive experts employed by CIA, or are we professional analysts and intelligence officers whose expertise lies in our ability to adapt quickly to diverse issues and problems and analyze them effectively? In the world at large, substantive expertise is far more abundant than expertise on analytic science and the human mental processing of information. *Dick Heuer makes clear that the pitfalls the human mental process sets for analysts cannot be eliminated; they are part of us. What can be done is to train people how to look for and recognize these mental obstacles, and how to develop procedures designed to offset them.*

Given the centrality of analytic science for the intelligence mission, a key question that Heuer's book poses is: Compared with other areas of our business, have we committed a commensurate effort to the study of analytic science as a professional requirement? How do the effort and resource commitments in this area compare to, for example, the effort and commitment to the development of analysts' writing skills?

Heuer's book does not pretend to be the last word on this issue. Hopefully, it will be a stimulant for much more work.

PREFACE

This volume pulls together and republishes, with some editing, updating, and additions, articles written during 1978-86 for internal use within the CIA Directorate of Intelligence. Four of the articles also appeared in the Intelligence Community journal *Studies in Intelligence* during that time frame. The information is relatively timeless and still relevant to the never-ending quest for better analysis.

The articles are based on reviewing cognitive psychology literature concerning how people process information to make judgments on incomplete and ambiguous information. I selected the experiments and findings that seem most relevant to intelligence analysis and most in need of communication to intelligence analysts. I then translated the technical reports into language that intelligence analysts can understand and interpreted the relevance of these findings to the problems intelligence analysts face.

The result is a compromise that may not be wholly satisfactory to either research psychologists or intelligence analysts. Cognitive psychologists and decision analysts may complain of oversimplification, while the non-psychologist reader may have to absorb some new terminology. Unfortunately, mental processes are so complex that discussion of them does require some specialized vocabulary. Intelligence analysts who have read and thought seriously about the nature of their craft should have no difficulty with this book. Those who are plowing virgin ground may require serious effort.

I wish to thank all those who contributed comments and suggestions on the draft of this book: Jack Davis (who also wrote the Introduction); four former Directorate of Intelligence (DI) analysts whose names cannot be cited here; my current colleague, Prof. Theodore Sarbin; and my editor at the CIA's Center for the Study of Intelligence, Hank Appelbaum. All made many substantive and editorial suggestions that helped greatly to make this a better book.

                                                    Richards J. Heuer, Jr.

INTRODUCTION: IMPROVING INTELLIGENCE ANALYSIS AT CIA: DICK HEUER'S CONTRIBUTION TO INTELLIGENCE ANALYSIS

Jack Davis [1]

SUMMARY

I applaud CIA's Center for the Study of Intelligence for making the work of Richards J. Heuer, Jr. on the psychology of intelligence analysis available to a new generation of intelligence practitioners and scholars.

Dick Heuer's ideas on how to improve analysis focus on helping analysts compensate for the human mind's limitations in dealing with complex problems that typically involve ambiguous information, multiple players, and fluid circumstances. Such multi-faceted estimative challenges have proliferated in the turbulent post-Cold War world.

Heuer's message to analysts can be encapsulated by quoting two sentences from Chapter 4 of this book:

Intelligence analysts should be self-conscious about their reasoning processes. They should think about *how* they make judgments and reach conclusions, not just about the judgments and conclusions themselves.

Heuer's ideas are applicable to any analytical endeavor. In this Introduction, I have concentrated on his impact--and that of other pioneer thinkers in the intelligence analysis field--at CIA, because that is the institution that Heuer and his predecessors, and I myself, know best, having spent the bulk of our intelligence careers there.

LEADING CONTRIBUTORS TO QUALITY OF ANALYSIS

Intelligence analysts, in seeking to make sound judgments, are always under challenge from the complexities of the issues they address and from the demands made on them for timeliness and volume of production. Four Agency individuals over the decades stand out for having made major contributions on how to deal with these challenges to the quality of analysis.

My short list of the people who have had the greatest positive impact on CIA analysis consists of Sherman Kent, Robert Gates, Douglas MacEachin, and Richards Heuer. My selection methodology was simple. I asked myself: Whose insights have influenced me the most during my four decades of practicing, teaching, and writing about analysis?

Sherman Kent

Sherman Kent's pathbreaking contributions to analysis cannot be done justice in a couple of paragraphs, and I refer readers to fuller treatments elsewhere.[2] Here I address his general legacy to the analytical profession.

Kent, a professor of European history at Yale, worked in the Research and Analysis branch of the Office of Strategic Services during World War II. He wrote an influential book, *Strategic Intelligence for American World Power,* while at the National War College in the late 1940s. He served as Vice Chairman and then as Chairman of the DCI's Board of National Estimates from 1950 to 1967.

Kent's greatest contribution to the quality of analysis was to define an honorable place for the analyst--the thoughtful individual "applying the instruments of reason and the scientific method"--in an intelligence world then as now dominated by collectors and operators. In a second (1965) edition of *Strategic Intelligence,* Kent took account of the coming computer age as well as human and technical collectors in proclaiming the centrality of the analyst:

Whatever the complexities of the puzzles we strive to solve and whatever the sophisticated techniques we may use to collect the pieces and store them, there can never be a time when the thoughtful man can be supplanted as the intelligence device supreme.

More specifically, Kent advocated application of the techniques of "scientific" study of the past to analysis of complex ongoing situations and estimates of likely future events. Just as rigorous "impartial" analysis could cut through the gaps and ambiguities of information on events long past and point to the most probable explanation, he contended, the powers of the critical mind could turn to events that had not yet transpired to determine the most probable developments.[3]

To this end, Kent developed the concept of the analytic pyramid, featuring a wide base of factual information and sides comprised of sound assumptions, which pointed to the most likely future scenario at the apex. [4]

In his proselytizing and in practice, Kent battled against bureaucratic and ideological biases, which he recognized as impediments to sound analysis, and against imprecise estimative terms that he saw as obstacles to conveying clear messages to readers. Although he was aware of what is now called cognitive bias, his writings urge analysts to "make the call" without much discussion of how limitations of the human mind were to be overcome.

Not many Agency analysts read Kent nowadays. But he had a profound impact on earlier generations of analysts and managers, and his work continues to exert an indirect influence among practitioners of the analytic profession.

Robert Gates

Bob Gates served as Deputy Director of Central Intelligence (1986-1989) and as DCI (1991-1993). But his greatest impact on the quality of CIA analysis came during his 1982-1986 stint as Deputy Director for Intelligence (DDI).

Initially schooled as a political scientist, Gates earned a Ph.D. in Soviet studies at Georgetown while working as an analyst at CIA. As a member of the National Security Council staff during the 1970s, he gained invaluable insight into how policymakers use intelligence analysis. Highly intelligent, exceptionally hard-working, and skilled in the bureaucratic arts, Gates was appointed DDI by DCI William Casey in good part because he was one of the few insiders Casey found who shared the DCI's views on what Casey saw as glaring deficiencies of Agency analysts. [5] Few analysts and managers who heard it have forgotten Gates' blistering criticism of analytic performance in his 1982 "inaugural" speech as DDI.

Most of the public commentary on Gates and Agency analysis concerned charges of politicization levied against him, and his defense against such charges, during Senate hearings for his 1991 confirmation as DCI. The heat of this debate was slow to dissipate among CIA analysts, as reflected in the pages of *Studies in Intelligence,* the Agency journal founded by Sherman Kent in the 1950s.[6]

I know of no written retrospective on Gates' contribution to Agency analysis. My insights into his ideas about analysis came mostly through an arms-length collaboration in setting up and running an Agency training course entitled "Seminar on Intelligence Successes and Failures."[7] During his tenure as DDI, only rarely could you hold a conversation with analysts or managers without picking up additional viewpoints, thoughtful and otherwise, on what Gates was doing to change CIA analysis.

Gates's ideas for overcoming what he saw as insular, flabby, and incoherent argumentation featured the importance of distinguishing between what analysts know and what they believe--that is, to make clear what is "fact" (or reliably reported information) and what is the analyst's opinion (which had to be persuasively supported with evidence). Among his other tenets were the need to seek the views of non-CIA experts, including academic specialists and policy officials, and to present alternate future scenarios.

Gates's main impact, though, came from practice--from his direct involvement in implementing his ideas. Using his authority as DDI, he reviewed critically almost all in-depth assessments and current intelligence articles *prior to publication.* With help from his deputy and two rotating assistants from the ranks of rising junior managers, Gates raised the standards for DDI review dramatically--in essence, from "looks good to me" to "show me your evidence."

As the many drafts Gates rejected were sent back to managers who had approved them--accompanied by the DDI's comments about inconsistency, lack of clarity, substantive bias, and poorly supported judgments--the whole chain of review became much more rigorous. Analysts and their managers raised their standards to avoid the pain of DDI rejection. Both career advancement and ego were at stake.

The rapid and sharp increase in attention paid by analysts and managers to the underpinnings for their substantive judgments probably was without precedent in the Agency's history. The longer term benefits of the intensified review process were more limited, however, because insufficient attention was given to clarifying *tradecraft* practices that would promote analytic soundness. More than one participant in the process observed that a lack of guidelines for meeting Gates's standards led to a large amount of "wheel-spinning."

Gates's impact, like Kent's, has to be seen on two planes. On the one hand, little that Gates wrote on the craft of analysis is read these days. But even though his pre-publication review process was discontinued under his successors, an enduring awareness of his standards still gives pause at jumping to conclusions to many managers and analysts who experienced his criticism first-hand.

Douglas MacEachin*

Doug MacEachin, DDI from 1993 to 1996, sought to provide an essential ingredient for ensuring implementation of sound analytic standards: *corporate tradecraft* standards for analysts. This new tradecraft was aimed in particular at ensuring that sufficient attention would be paid to cognitive challenges in assessing complex issues.

MacEachin set out his views on Agency analytical faults and correctives in *The Tradecraft of Analysis: Challenge and Change in the CIA*.[8] My commentary on his contributions to sound analysis is also informed by a series of exchanges with him in 1994 and 1995.

MacEachin's university major was economics, but he also showed great interest in philosophy. His Agency career--like Gates'--included an extended assignment to a policymaking office. He came away from this experience with new insights on what constitutes "value-added" intelligence usable by policymakers. Subsequently, as CIA's senior manager on arms control issues, he dealt regularly with a cadre of tough-minded policy officials who let him know in blunt terms what worked as effective policy support and what did not.

By the time MacEachin became DDI in 1993, Gates's policy of DDI front-office pre-publication review of nearly all DI analytical studies had been discontinued. MacEachin took a different approach; he read--mostly on weekends--and reflected on numerous already-published DI analytical papers. He did not like what he found. In his words, roughly a third of the papers meant to assist the policymaking process had no discernible argumentation to bolster the credibility of intelligence judgments, and another third suffered from flawed argumentation. This experience, along with pressures on CIA for better analytic performance in the wake of alleged

---

* Douglas MacEachin is a former CIA Deputy Director of Intelligence. After 32 years with the Agency, he retired in 1997 and became a Senior Fellow at Harvard University's John F. Kennedy School of Government.

"intelligence failures" concerning Iraq's invasion of Kuwait, prompted his decision to launch a major new effort to raise analytical standards.[9]

MacEachin advocated an approach to structured argumentation called "linchpin analysis," to which he contributed muscular terms designed to overcome many CIA professionals' distaste for academic nomenclature. The standard academic term "key variables" became *drivers*. "Hypotheses" concerning drivers became *linchpins*--assumptions underlying the argument--and these had to be explicitly spelled out. MacEachin also urged that greater attention be paid to analytical processes for alerting policymakers to changes in circumstances that would increase the likelihood of alternative scenarios.

MacEachin thus worked to put in place systematic and transparent standards for determining whether analysts had met their responsibilities for critical thinking. To spread understanding and application of the standards, he mandated creation of workshops on linchpin analysis for managers and production of a series of notes on analytical tradecraft. He also directed that the DI's performance on tradecraft standards be tracked and that recognition be given to exemplary assessments. Perhaps most ambitious, he saw to it that instruction on standards for analysis was incorporated into a new training course, "Tradecraft 2000." Nearly all DI managers and analysts attended this course during 1996-97.

As of this writing (early 1999), the long-term staying power of MacEachin's tradecraft initiatives is not yet clear. But much of what he advocated has endured so far. Many DI analysts use variations on his linchpin concept to produce soundly argued forecasts. In the training realm, "Tradecraft 2000" has been supplanted by a new course that teaches the same concepts to newer analysts. But examples of what MacEachin would label as poorly substantiated analysis are still seen. Clearly, ongoing vigilance is needed to keep such analysis from finding its way into DI products.

Richards Heuer

Dick Heuer was--and is--much less well known within the CIA than Kent, Gates, and MacEachin. He has not received the wide acclaim that Kent enjoyed as the father of professional analysis, and he has lacked the bureaucratic powers that Gates and MacEachin could wield as DDIs. But his impact on the quality of Agency analysis arguably has been at least as important as theirs.

Heuer received a degree in philosophy in 1950 from Williams College, where, he notes, he became fascinated with the fundamental epistemological question, "What is truth and how can we know it?" In 1951, while a graduate student at the University of California's Berkeley campus, he was recruited as part of the CIA's buildup during the Korean War. The recruiter was Richard Helms, OSS veteran and rising player in the Agency's clandestine service. Future DCI Helms, according to Heuer, was looking for candidates for CIA employment among recent graduates of Williams College, his own alma mater. Heuer had an added advantage as a former editor of the college's newspaper, a position Helms had held some 15 years earlier.[10]

In 1975, after 24 years in the Directorate of Operations, Heuer moved to the DI. His earlier academic interest in how we know the truth was rekindled by two experiences. One was his involvement in the controversial case of Soviet KGB defector Yuriy Nosenko. The other was learning new approaches to social science methodology while earning a Master's degree in international relations at the University of Southern California's European campus.

At the time he retired in 1979, Heuer headed the methodology unit in the DI's political analysis office. He originally prepared most of the chapters in this book as individual articles between 1978 and 1986; many of them were written for the DI after his retirement. He has updated the articles and prepared some new material for inclusion in this book.

Heuer's Central Ideas

Dick Heuer's writings make three fundamental points about the cognitive challenges intelligence analysts face:

The mind is poorly "wired" to deal effectively with both inherent uncertainty (the natural fog surrounding complex, indeterminate intelligence issues) and induced uncertainty (the man-made fog fabricated by denial and deception operations).

Even increased awareness of cognitive and other "unmotivated" biases, such as the tendency to see information confirming an already-held judgment more vividly than one sees "disconfirming" information, does little by itself to help analysts deal effectively with uncertainty.

Tools and techniques that gear the analyst's mind to apply higher levels of critical thinking can substantially improve analysis on complex issues on which information is incomplete, ambiguous, and often deliberately distorted. Key examples of such intellectual devices include techniques for structuring information, challenging assumptions, and exploring alternative interpretations.

The following passage from Heuer's 1980 article entitled "Perception: Why Can't We See What Is There to be Seen?" shows that his ideas were similar to or compatible with MacEachin's concepts of linchpin analysis.

Given the difficulties inherent in the human processing of complex information, a prudent management system should:

- Encourage products that (a) clearly delineate their assumptions and chains of inference and (b) specify the degree and source of the uncertainty involved in the conclusions.
- Emphasize procedures that expose and elaborate alternative points of view--analytic debates, devil's advocates, interdisciplinary brainstorming, competitive analysis, intra-office peer review of production, and elicitation of outside expertise.

Heuer emphasizes both the value and the dangers of *mental models,* or *mind-sets.* In the book's opening chapter, entitled "Thinking About Thinking," he notes that:

[Analysts] construct their own version of "reality" on the basis of information provided by the senses, but this sensory input is mediated by complex mental processes that determine which information is attended to, how it is organized, and the meaning attributed to it. What people perceive, how readily they perceive it, and how they process this information after receiving it are all strongly influenced by past experience, education, cultural values, role requirements, and organizational norms, as well as by the specifics of the information received.

This process may be visualized as perceiving the world through a lens or screen that channels and focuses and thereby may distort the images that are seen. To achieve the clearest possible image...analysts need more than information...They also need to understand the lenses through which this information passes. These lenses are known by many terms--mental models, mind-sets, biases, or analytic assumptions.

In essence, Heuer sees reliance on mental models to simplify and interpret reality as an unavoidable conceptual mechanism for intelligence analysts--often useful, but at times hazardous. What is required of analysts, in his view, is a commitment to *challenge, refine, and challenge again* their own working mental models, precisely because these steps are central to sound interpretation of complex and ambiguous issues.

Throughout the book, Heuer is critical of the orthodox prescription of "more and better information" to remedy unsatisfactory analytic performance. He urges that greater attention be paid instead to more intensive exploitation of information already on hand, and that in so doing, analysts continuously challenge and revise their mental models.

Heuer sees *mirror-imaging* as an example of an unavoidable cognitive trap. No matter how much expertise an analyst applies to interpreting the value systems of foreign entities, when the hard evidence runs out the tendency to project the analyst's own mind-set takes over. In Chapter 4, Heuer observes:

To see the options faced by foreign leaders as these leaders see them, one must understand their values and assumptions and even their misperceptions and misunderstandings. Without such insight, interpreting foreign leaders' decisions or forecasting future decisions is often nothing more than partially informed speculation. Too frequently, foreign behavior appears "irrational" or "not in their own best interest." Such conclusions often indicate analysts have projected American values and conceptual frameworks onto the foreign leaders and societies, rather than understanding the logic of the situation as it appears to them.

Competing Hypotheses

To offset the risks accompanying analysts' inevitable recourse to mirror-imaging, Heuer suggests looking upon analysts' calculations about foreign beliefs and behavior as hypotheses to be challenged. Alternative hypotheses need to be carefully considered--especially those that cannot be *disproved* on the basis of available information.

Heuer's concept of "Analysis of Competing Hypotheses" (ACH) is among his most important contributions to the development of an intelligence analysis methodology. At the core of ACH is the notion of competition among a series of plausible hypotheses to see which ones survive a gauntlet of testing for compatibility with available information. The surviving hypotheses--those that have not been disproved--are subjected to further testing. ACH, Heuer concedes, will not always yield the right answer. But it can help analysts overcome the cognitive limitations discussed in his book.

Some analysts who use ACH follow Heuer's full eight-step methodology. More often, they employ some elements of ACH--especially the use of available information to challenge the hypotheses that the analyst favors the most.

Denial and Deception

Heuer's path-breaking work on countering denial and deception (D&D) was not included as a separate chapter in this volume. But his brief references here are persuasive.

He notes, for example, that analysts often reject the possibility of deception because they see no evidence of it. He then argues that rejection is not justified under these circumstances. If deception is well planned and properly executed, one should not expect to see evidence of it readily at hand. Rejecting a plausible but unproven hypothesis too early tends to bias the subsequent analysis, because one does not then look for the evidence that might support it. The possibility of deception should not be rejected until it is disproved or, at least, until a systematic search for evidence has been made and none has been found.

HEUER'S IMPACT

Heuer's influence on analytic tradecraft began with his first articles. CIA officials who set up training courses in the 1980s as part of then-DDI Gates's quest for improved analysis shaped their lesson plans partly on the basis of Heuer's findings. Among these courses were a seminar on intelligence successes and failures and another on intelligence analysis. The courses influenced scores of DI analysts, many of whom are now in the managerial ranks. The designers and teachers of Tradecraft 2000 clearly were also influenced by Heuer, as reflected in reading selections, case studies, and class exercises.

Heuer's work has remained on reading lists and in lesson plans for DI training courses offered to all new analysts, as well as courses on warning analysis and on countering denial and deception. Senior analysts and managers who have been directly exposed to Heuer's thinking through his articles, or through training courses, continue to pass his insights on to newer analysts.

RECOMMENDATIONS

Heuer's advice to Agency leaders, managers, and analysts is pointed: To ensure sustained improvement in assessing complex issues, analysis must be treated as more than a substantive and organizational process. Attention also must be paid to techniques and tools for coping with the inherent limitations on analysts' mental machinery. He urges that Agency leaders take steps to:

- *Establish an organizational environment* that promotes and rewards the kind of critical thinking he advocates--or example, analysis on difficult issues that considers in depth a series of plausible hypotheses rather than allowing the first credible hypothesis to suffice.
- *Expand funding for research* on the role such mental processes play in shaping analytical judgments. An Agency that relies on sharp cognitive performance by its analysts must stay abreast of studies on how the mind works--i.e., on *how* analysts reach judgments.
- *Foster development of tools* to assist analysts in assessing information. On tough issues, they need help in improving their mental models and in deriving incisive findings from information they already have; they need such help at least as much as they need more information.

I offer some concluding observations and recommendations, rooted in Heuer's findings and taking into account the tough tradeoffs facing intelligence professionals:

- *Commit to a uniform set of tradecraft standards based on the insights in this book.* Leaders need to know if analysts have done their cognitive homework before taking corporate responsibility for their judgments. Although every analytical issue can be seen as one of a kind, I suspect that nearly all such topics fit into about a dozen recurring patterns of challenge based largely on variations in substantive uncertainty and policy sensitivity. Corporate standards need to be established for each such category. And the burden should be put on managers to explain why a given analytical assignment requires deviation from the standards. I am convinced that if tradecraft standards are made uniform and transparent, the time saved by curtailing personalistic review of quick-turnaround analysis (e.g., "It reads better to me this way") could be "reinvested" in doing battle more effectively against cognitive pitfalls. ("Regarding point 3, let's talk about your assumptions.")

- *Pay more honor to "doubt."* Intelligence leaders and policymakers should, in recognition of the cognitive impediments to sound analysis, establish ground rules that enable analysts, after doing their best to clarify an issue, to express doubts more openly. They should be encouraged to list gaps in information and other obstacles to confident judgment. Such conclusions as "We do not know" or "There are several potentially valid ways to assess this issue" should be regarded as badges of sound analysis, not as dereliction of analytic duty.

- Find a couple of successors to Dick Heuer. Fund their research. Heed their findings.

PART I:
OUR MENTAL MACHINERY

Chapter 1

THINKING ABOUT THINKING

SUMMARY

Of the diverse problems that impede accurate intelligence analysis, those inherent in human mental processes are surely among the most important and most difficult to deal with. Intelligence analysis is fundamentally a mental process, but understanding this process is hindered by the lack of conscious awareness of the workings of our own minds.

A basic finding of cognitive psychology is that people have no conscious experience of most of what happens in the human mind. Many functions associated with perception, memory, and information processing are conducted prior to and independently of any conscious direction. What appears spontaneously in consciousness is the result of thinking, not the process of thinking.

Weaknesses and biases inherent in human thinking processes can be demonstrated through carefully designed experiments. They can be alleviated by conscious application of tools and techniques that should be in the analytical tradecraft toolkit of all intelligence analysts.

"When we speak of improving the mind we are usually referring to the acquisition of information or knowledge, or to the type of thoughts one should have, and not to the actual functioning of the mind. We spend little time monitoring our own thinking and comparing it with a more sophisticated ideal." [11]

When we speak of improving intelligence analysis, we are usually referring to the quality of writing, types of analytical products, relations between intelligence analysts and intelligence consumers, or organization of the analytical process. Little attention is devoted to improving how analysts think.

Thinking analytically is a skill like carpentry or driving a car. It can be taught, it can be learned, and it can improve with practice. But like many other skills, such as riding a bike, it is not learned by sitting in a classroom and being told how to do it. Analysts learn by doing. Most people achieve at least a minimally acceptable level of analytical performance with little conscious effort beyond completing their education. With much effort and hard work, however, analysts can achieve a level of excellence beyond what comes naturally.

Regular running enhances endurance but does not improve technique without expert guidance. Similarly, expert guidance may be required to modify long-established analytical habits to achieve an optimal level of analytical excellence. An analytical coaching staff to help young analysts hone their analytical tradecraft would be a valuable supplement to classroom instruction.

One key to successful learning is motivation. Some of CIA's best analysts developed their skills as a consequence of experiencing analytical failure early in their careers. Failure motivated them to be more self-conscious about how they do analysis and to sharpen their thinking process.

This book aims to help intelligence analysts achieve a higher level of performance. It shows how people make judgments based on incomplete and ambiguous information, and it offers simple tools and concepts for improving analytical skills.

Part I identifies some limitations inherent in human mental processes. Part II discusses analytical tradecraft--simple tools and approaches for overcoming these limitations and thinking more systematically. Chapter 8, "Analysis of Competing Hypotheses," is arguably the most important single chapter. Part III presents information about cognitive biases--the technical term for predictable mental errors caused by simplified information processing strategies. A final chapter presents a checklist for analysts and recommendations for how managers of intelligence analysis can help create an environment in which analytical excellence flourishes.

Herbert Simon first advanced the concept of "bounded" or limited rationality.[12] Because of limits in human mental capacity, he argued, the mind cannot cope directly with the complexity of the world. Rather, we construct a simplified mental model of reality and then work with this model. We behave rationally within the confines of our mental model, but this model is not always well adapted to the requirements of the real world. The concept of bounded rationality has come to be recognized widely, though not universally, both as an accurate portrayal of human judgment and choice and as a sensible adjustment to the limitations inherent in how the human mind functions.[13]

Much psychological research on perception, memory, attention span, and reasoning capacity documents the limitations in our "mental machinery" identified by Simon. Many scholars have applied these psychological insights to the study of international political behavior.[14] A similar psychological perspective underlies some writings on intelligence failure and strategic surprise.[15]

This book differs from those works in two respects. It analyzes problems from the perspective of intelligence analysts rather than policymakers. And it documents the impact of mental processes largely through experiments in cognitive psychology rather than through examples from diplomatic and military history.

A central focus of this book is to illuminate the role of the observer in determining what is observed and how it is interpreted. People construct their own version of "reality" on the basis of information provided by the senses, but this sensory input is mediated by complex mental processes that determine which information is attended to, how it is organized, and the meaning attributed to it. What people perceive, how readily they perceive it, and how they process this information after receiving it are all strongly influenced by past experience, education, cultural values, role requirements, and organizational norms, as well as by the specifics of the information received.

This process may be visualized as perceiving the world through a lens or screen that channels and focuses and thereby may distort the images that are seen. To achieve the clearest possible image of China, for example, analysts need more than information on China. They also need to understand their own lenses through which this information passes. These lenses are known by many terms--mental models, mind-sets, biases, or analytical assumptions.

In this book, the terms mental model and mind-set are used more or less interchangeably, although a mental model is likely to be better developed and articulated than a mind-set. An analytical assumption is one part of a mental model or mind-set. The biases discussed in this book result from how the mind works and are independent of any substantive mental model or mind-set.

Before obtaining a license to practice, psychoanalysts are required to undergo psychoanalysis themselves in order to become more aware of how their own personality interacts with and conditions their observations of others. The practice of psychoanalysis has not been so successful that its procedures should be emulated by the intelligence and foreign policy community. But the analogy highlights an interesting point: Intelligence analysts must understand themselves before they can understand others. Training is needed to (a) increase self-awareness concerning generic problems in how people perceive and make analytical judgments concerning foreign events, and (b) provide guidance and practice in overcoming these problems.

Not enough training is focused in this direction--that is, inward toward the analyst's own thought processes. Training of intelligence analysts generally means instruction in organizational procedures, methodological techniques, or substantive topics. More training time should be devoted to the mental act of thinking or analyzing. It is simply assumed, incorrectly, that analysts know how to analyze. This book is intended to support training that examines the thinking and reasoning processes involved in intelligence analysis.

As discussed in the next chapter, mind-sets and mental models are inescapable. They are, in essence, a distillation of all that we think we know about a subject. The problem is how to ensure that the mind remains open to alternative interpretations in a rapidly changing world.

The disadvantage of a mind-set is that it can color and control our perception to the extent that an experienced specialist may be among the last to see what is really happening when events take a new and unexpected turn. When faced with a major paradigm shift, analysts who know the most about a subject have the most to unlearn. This seems to have happened before the reunification of Germany, for example. Some German specialists had to be prodded by their more generalist supervisors to accept the significance of the dramatic changes in progress toward reunification of East and West Germany.

The advantage of mind-sets is that they help analysts get the production out on time and keep things going effectively between those watershed events that become chapter headings in the history books.[16]

A generation ago, few intelligence analysts were self-conscious and introspective about the process by which they did analysis. The accepted wisdom was the "common sense" theory of knowledge--that to perceive events accurately it was necessary only to open one's eyes, look at the facts, and purge oneself of all preconceptions and prejudices in order to make an objective judgment.

Today, there is greatly increased understanding that intelligence analysts do not approach their tasks with empty minds. They start with a set of assumptions about how events normally transpire in the area for which they are responsible. Although this changed view is becoming conventional wisdom, the Intelligence Community has only begun to scratch the surface of its implications.

If analysts' understanding of events is greatly influenced by the mind-set or mental model through which they perceive those events, should there not be more research to explore and document the impact of different mental models?[17]

The reaction of the Intelligence Community to many problems is to collect more information, even though analysts in many cases already have more information than they can digest. What analysts need is more truly useful information--mostly reliable HUMINT from knowledgeable insiders-- to help them make good decisions. Or they need a more accurate mental model and better analytical tools to help them sort through, make sense of, and get the most out of the available ambiguous and conflicting information.

Psychological research also offers to intelligence analysts additional insights that are beyond the scope of this book. Problems are not limited to how analysts perceive and process information. Intelligence analysts often work in small groups and always within the context of a large, bureaucratic organization. Problems are inherent in the processes that occur at all three levels--individual, small group, and organization. This book focuses on problems inherent in analysts' mental processes, inasmuch as these are probably the most insidious. Analysts can observe and get a feel for these problems in small-group and organizational processes, but it is very difficult, at best, to be self-conscious about the workings of one's own mind.

Chapter 2

PERCEPTION: WHY CAN'T WE SEE WHAT IS THERE TO BE SEEN?

SUMMARY

The process of perception links people to their environment and is critical to accurate understanding of the world about us. Accurate intelligence analysis obviously requires accurate perception. Yet research into human perception demonstrates that the process is beset by many pitfalls. Moreover, the circumstances under which intelligence analysis is conducted are precisely the circumstances in which accurate perception tends to be most difficult. This chapter discusses perception in general, then applies this information to illuminate some of the difficulties of intelligence analysis.[18]

People tend to think of perception as a passive process. We see, hear, smell, taste or feel stimuli that impinge upon our senses. We think that if we are at all objective, we record what is actually there. Yet perception is demonstrably an active rather than a passive process; it constructs rather than records "reality." Perception implies understanding as well as awareness. It is a process of inference in which people construct their own version of reality on the basis of information provided through the five senses.

As already noted, what people in general and analysts in particular perceive, and how readily they perceive it, are strongly influenced by their past experience, education, cultural values, and role requirements, as well as by the stimuli recorded by their receptor organs.

Many experiments have been conducted to show the extraordinary extent to which the information obtained by an observer depends upon the observer's own assumptions and preconceptions. For example, when you looked at Figure 1 below, what did you see? Now refer to the footnote for a description of what is actually there [19]. Did you perceive Figure 1 correctly? If so, you have exceptional powers of observation, were lucky, or have seen the figure before. This simple experiment demonstrates one of the most fundamental principles concerning perception:

Figure 1

We tend to perceive what we expect to perceive.

A corollary of this principle is that it takes more information, and more unambiguous information, to recognize an unexpected phenomenon than an expected one.

One classic experiment to demonstrate the influence of expectations on perception used playing cards, some of which were gimmicked so the spades were red and the hearts black. Pictures of the cards were flashed briefly on a screen and, needless to say, the test subjects identified the normal cards more quickly and accurately than the anomalous ones. After test subjects became aware of the existence of red spades and black hearts, their performance with the gimmicked cards improved but still did not approach the speed or accuracy with which normal cards could be identified.[20]

This experiment shows that patterns of expectation become so deeply embedded that they continue to influence perceptions even when people are alerted to and try to take account of the existence of data that do not fit their preconceptions. Trying to be objective does not ensure accurate perception.

The position of the test subject identifying playing cards is analogous to that of the intelligence analyst or government leader trying to make sense of the paper flow that crosses his or her desk. What is actually perceived in that paper flow, as well as how it is interpreted, depends in part, at least, on the analyst's patterns of expectation. Analysts do not just have expectations about the color of hearts and spades. They have a set of assumptions and expectations about the motivations of people and the processes of government in foreign countries. Events consistent with these expectations are perceived and processed easily, while events that contradict prevailing expectations tend to be ignored or distorted in perception. Of course, this distortion is a subconscious or pre-conscious process, as illustrated by how you presumably ignored the extra words in the triangles in Figure 1.

This tendency of people to perceive what they *expect* to perceive is more important than any tendency to perceive what they *want* to perceive. In fact, there may be no real tendency toward wishful thinking. The commonly cited evidence supporting the claim that people tend to perceive what they want to perceive can generally be explained equally well by the expectancy thesis.[21]

Expectations have many diverse sources, including past experience, professional training, and cultural and organizational norms. All these influences predispose analysts to pay particular attention to certain kinds of information and to organize and interpret this information in certain ways. Perception is also influenced by the context in which it occurs. Different circumstances evoke different sets of expectations. People are more attuned to hearing footsteps behind them when walking in an alley at night than along a city street in daytime, and the meaning attributed to the sound of footsteps will vary under these differing circumstances. A military intelligence analyst may be similarly tuned to perceive indicators of potential conflict.

Patterns of expectations tell analysts, subconsciously, what to look for, what is important, and how to interpret what is seen. These patterns form a mind-set that predisposes analysts to think in certain ways. A mind-set is akin to a screen or lens through which one perceives the world.

There is a tendency to think of a mind-set as something bad, to be avoided. According to this line of argument, one should have an open mind and be influenced only by the facts rather than by preconceived notions! That is an unreachable ideal. There is no such thing as "the facts of the case." There is only a very selective subset of the overall mass of data to which one has been subjected that one takes as facts and judges to be relevant to the question at issue.

Actually, mind-sets are neither good nor bad; they are unavoidable. People have no conceivable way of coping with the volume of stimuli that impinge upon their senses, or with the volume and complexity of the data they have to analyze, without some kind of simplifying preconceptions about what to expect, what is important, and what is related to what. "There is a grain of truth in the otherwise pernicious maxim that an open mind is an empty mind."[22] Analysts do not achieve objective analysis by avoiding preconceptions; that would be ignorance or self-delusion. Objectivity is achieved by making basic assumptions and reasoning as explicit as possible so that they can be challenged by others and analysts can, themselves, examine their validity.

One of the most important characteristics of mind-sets is:
Mind-sets tend to be quick to form but resistant to change.

Impressions resist change.

Figure 2

Figure 2 illustrates this principle by showing part of a longer series of progressively modified drawings that change almost imperceptibly from a man into a woman.[23] The right-hand drawing in the top row, when viewed alone, has equal chances of being perceived as a man or a woman. When test subjects are shown the entire series of drawings one by one, their perception of this intermediate drawing is biased according to which end of the series they started from. Test subjects who start by viewing a picture that is clearly a man are biased in favor of continuing to see a man long after an "objective observer" (for example, an observer who has seen only a single picture) recognizes that the man is now a woman. Similarly, test subjects who start at the woman end of the series are biased in favor of continuing to see a woman. Once an observer has formed an image--that is, once he or she has developed a mind-set or expectation concerning the phenomenon being observed--this conditions future perceptions of that phenomenon.

This is the basis for another general principle of perception:
New information is assimilated to existing images.

This principle explains why gradual, evolutionary change often goes unnoticed. It also explains the phenomenon that an intelligence analyst assigned to work on a topic or country for the first time may generate accurate insights that have been overlooked by experienced analysts who have worked on the same problem for 10 years. A fresh perspective is sometimes useful; past experience can handicap as well as aid analysis. This tendency to assimilate new data into pre-existing images is greater "the more ambiguous the information, the more confident the actor is of the validity of his image, and the greater his commitment to the established view."[24]

It is difficult to look at the same information from different perspectives.

Figure 3

The drawing in Figure 3 provides the reader an opportunity to test for him or herself the persistence of established images.[25] Look at Figure 3. What do you see--an old woman or a young woman? Now look again to see if you can visually and mentally reorganize the data to form a different image--that of a young woman if your original perception was of an old woman, or of the old woman if you first perceived the young one. If necessary, look at the footnote for clues to help you identify the other image.[26] Again, this exercise illustrates the principle that mind-sets are quick to form but resistant to change.

When you have seen Figure 3 from *both* perspectives, try shifting back and forth from one perspective to the other. Do you notice some initial difficulty in making this switch? One of the more difficult mental feats is to take a familiar body of data and reorganize it visually or mentally to perceive it from a different perspective. Yet this is what intelligence analysts are constantly required to do. In order to understand international interactions, analysts must understand the situation as it appears to each of the opposing forces, and constantly shift back and forth from one perspective to the other as they try to fathom how each side interprets an ongoing series of interactions. Trying to perceive an adversary's interpretations of international events, as well as US interpretations of those same events, is comparable to seeing both the old and young woman in Figure 3. Once events have been perceived one way, there is a natural resistance to other perspectives.

A related point concerns the impact of substandard conditions of perception. The basic principle is:

Initial exposure to blurred or ambiguous stimuli interferes with accurate perception even after more and better information becomes available.

This effect has been demonstrated experimentally by projecting onto a screen pictures of common, everyday subjects such as a dog standing on grass, a fire hydrant, and an aerial view of a highway cloverleaf intersection.[27] The initial projection was blurred in varying degrees, and the pictures were then brought into focus slowly to determine at what point test subjects could identify them correctly.

This experiment showed two things. First, those who started viewing the pictures when they were most out of focus had more difficulty identifying them when they became clearer than those who started viewing at a less blurred stage. In other words, the greater the initial blur, the clearer the picture had to be before people could recognize it. Second, the longer people were exposed to a blurred picture, the clearer the picture had to be before they could recognize it.

What happened in this experiment is what presumably happens in real life; despite ambiguous stimuli, people form some sort of tentative hypothesis about what they see. The longer they are exposed to this blurred image, the greater confidence they develop in this initial and perhaps erroneous impression, so the greater the impact this initial impression has on subsequent perceptions. For a time, as the picture becomes clearer, there is no *obvious* contradiction; the new data are assimilated into the previous image, and the initial interpretation is maintained until the contradiction becomes so obvious that it forces itself upon our consciousness.

The early but incorrect impression tends to persist because the amount of information necessary to invalidate a hypothesis is considerably greater than the amount of information required to make an initial interpretation. The problem is not that there is any inherent difficulty in grasping new perceptions or new ideas, but that established perceptions are so difficult to change. People form impressions on the basis of very little information, but once formed, they do not reject or change them unless they obtain rather solid evidence. Analysts might seek to limit the adverse impact of this tendency by suspending judgment for as long as possible as new information is being received.

IMPLICATIONS FOR INTELLIGENCE ANALYSIS

Comprehending the nature of perception has significant implications for understanding the nature and limitations of intelligence analysis. The circumstances under which accurate perception is most difficult are exactly the circumstances under which intelligence analysis is generally conducted-- dealing with highly ambiguous situations on the basis of information that is processed incrementally under pressure for early judgment. This is a recipe for inaccurate perception.

Intelligence seeks to illuminate the unknown. Almost by definition, intelligence analysis deals with highly ambiguous situations. As previously noted, the greater the ambiguity of the stimuli, the greater the impact of expectations and pre-existing images on the perception of that stimuli. Thus, despite maximum striving for objectivity, the intelligence analyst's own preconceptions are likely to exert a greater impact on the analytical product than in other fields where an analyst is working with less ambiguous and less discordant information.

Moreover, the intelligence analyst is among the first to look at new problems at an early stage when the evidence is very fuzzy indeed. The analyst then follows a problem as additional increments of evidence are received and the picture gradually clarifies--as happened with test subjects in the experiment demonstrating that initial exposure to blurred stimuli interferes with accurate perception even after more and better information becomes available. If the results of this experiment can be generalized to apply to intelligence analysts, the experiment suggests that an analyst who starts observing a potential problem situation at an early and unclear stage is at a disadvantage as compared with others, such as policymakers, whose first exposure may come at a later stage when more and better information is available.

The receipt of information in small increments over time also facilitates assimilation of this information into the analyst's existing views. No one item of information may be sufficient to prompt the analyst to change a previous view. The cumulative message inherent in many pieces of information may be significant but is attenuated when this information is not examined as a whole. The Intelligence Community's review of its performance before the 1973 Arab-Israeli War noted:

The problem of incremental analysis--especially as it applies to the current intelligence process--was also at work in the period preceding hostilities. Analysts, according to their own accounts, were often proceeding on the basis of the day's take, hastily comparing it with material received the previous day. They then produced in 'assembly line fashion' items which may have reflected perceptive intuition but which [did not] accrue from a systematic consideration of an accumulated body of integrated evidence.[28]

And finally, the intelligence analyst operates in an environment that exerts strong pressures for what psychologists call premature closure. Customer demand for interpretive analysis is greatest within two or three days after an event occurs. The system requires the intelligence analyst to come up with an almost instant diagnosis before sufficient hard information, and the broader background information that may be needed to gain perspective, become available to make possible a well-grounded judgment. This diagnosis can only be based upon the analyst's preconceptions concerning how and why events normally transpire in a given society.

As time passes and more information is received, a fresh look at all the evidence might suggest a different explanation. Yet, the perception experiments indicate that an early judgment adversely affects the formation of future perceptions. Once an observer thinks he or she knows what is happening, this perception tends to resist change. New data received incrementally can be fit easily into an analyst's previous image. This perceptual bias is reinforced by organizational pressures favoring consistent interpretation; once the analyst is committed in writing, both the analyst and the organization have a vested interest in maintaining the original assessment.

That intelligence analysts perform as well as they do is testimony to their generally sound judgment, training, and dedication in performing a dauntingly difficult task.

The problems outlined here have implications for the management as well as the conduct of analysis. Given the difficulties inherent in the human processing of complex information, a prudent management system should:

Encourage products that clearly delineate their assumptions and chains of inference and that specify the degree and source of uncertainty involved in the conclusions.

Support analyses that periodically re-examine key problems from the ground up in order to avoid the pitfalls of the incremental approach.

Emphasize procedures that expose and elaborate alternative points of view.

Educate consumers about the limitations as well as the capabilities of intelligence analysis; define a set of realistic expectations as a standard against which to judge analytical performance.

Chapter 3

MEMORY: HOW DO WE REMEMBER WHAT WE KNOW?

SUMMARY

Differences between stronger and weaker analytical performance are attributable in large measure to differences in the organization of data and experience in analysts' long-term memory. The contents of memory form a continuous input into the analytical process, and anything that influences what information is remembered or retrieved from memory also influences the outcome of analysis.

This chapter discusses the capabilities and limitations of several components of the memory system. Sensory information storage and short-term memory are beset by severe limitations of capacity, while long-term memory, for all practical purposes, has a virtually infinite capacity. With long-term memory, the problems concern getting information into it and retrieving information once it is there, not physical limits on the amount of information that may be stored. Understanding how memory works provides insight into several analytical strengths and weaknesses.

COMPONENTS OF THE MEMORY SYSTEM

What is commonly called memory is not a single, simple function. It is an extraordinarily complex system of diverse components and processes. There are at least three, and very likely more, distinct memory processes. The most important from the standpoint of this discussion and best documented by scientific research are sensory information storage (SIS), short-term memory (STM), and long-term memory (LTM).[29] Each differs with respect to function, the form of information held, the length of time information is retained, and the amount of information-handling capacity. Memory researchers also posit the existence of an interpretive mechanism and an overall memory monitor or control mechanism that guides interaction among various elements of the memory system.

Sensory Information Storage

Sensory information storage holds sensory images for several tenths of a second after they are received by the sensory organs. The functioning of SIS may be observed if you close your eyes, then open and close them again as rapidly as possible. As your eyes close, notice how the visual image is maintained for a fraction of a second before fading. Sensory information storage explains why a movie film shot at 16 separate frames per second appears as continuous movement rather than a series of still pictures. A visual trace is generally retained in SIS for about one-quarter of a second. It is not possible to consciously extend the time that sensory information is held in SIS. The function of SIS is to make it possible for the brain to work on processing a sensory event for longer than the duration of the event itself.

Short-term Memory

Information passes from SIS into short-term memory, where again it is held for only a short period of time--a few seconds or minutes. Whereas SIS holds the complete image, STM stores only the interpretation of the image. If a sentence is spoken, SIS retains the sounds, while STM holds the words formed by these sounds.

Like SIS, short-term memory holds information temporarily, pending further processing. This processing includes judgments concerning meaning, relevance, and significance, as well as the mental actions necessary to integrate selected portions of the information into long-term memory. When a person forgets immediately the name of someone to whom he or she has just been introduced, it is because the name was not transferred from short-term to long-term memory.

A central characteristic of STM is the severe limitation on its capacity. A person who is asked to listen to and repeat a series of 10 or 20 names or numbers normally retains only five or six items. Commonly it is the last five or six. If one focuses instead on the first items, STM becomes saturated by this effort, and the person cannot concentrate on and recall the last items. People make a choice where to focus their attention. They can concentrate on remembering or interpreting or taking notes on information received moments ago, or pay attention to information currently being received. Limitations on the capacity of short-term memory often preclude doing both.

Retrieval of information from STM is direct and immediate because the information has never left the conscious mind. Information can be maintained in STM indefinitely by a process of "rehearsal"--repeating it over and over again. But while rehearsing some items to retain them in STM, people cannot simultaneously add new items. The severe limitation on the amount of information retainable in STM at any one time is physiological, and there is no way to overcome it. This is an important point that will be discussed below in connection with working memory and the utility of external memory aids.

Long-Term Memory

Some information retained in STM is processed into long-term memory. This information on past experiences is filed away in the recesses of the mind and must be retrieved before it can be used. In contrast to the immediate recall of current experience from STM, retrieval of information from LTM is indirect and sometimes laborious.

Loss of detail as sensory stimuli are interpreted and passed from SIS into STM and then into LTM is the basis for the phenomenon of selective perception discussed in the previous chapter. It imposes limits on subsequent stages of analysis, inasmuch as the lost data can never be retrieved. People can never take their mind back to what was *actually there* in sensory information storage or short-term memory. They can only retrieve their interpretation of what they *thought* was there as stored in LTM.

There are no practical limits to the amount of information that may be stored in LTM. The limitations of LTM are the difficulty of processing information into it and retrieving information from it. These subjects are discussed below.

The three memory processes comprise the storehouse of information or database that we call memory, but the total memory system must include other features as well. Some mental process must determine what information is passed from SIS into STM and from STM into LTM; decide how to search the LTM data base and judge whether further memory search is likely to be productive; assess the relevance of retrieved information; and evaluate potentially contradictory data.

To explain the operation of the total memory system, psychologists posit the existence of an interpretive mechanism that operates on the data base and a monitor or central control mechanism that guides and oversees the operation of the whole system. Little is known of these mechanisms and how they relate to other mental processes.

Despite much research on memory, little agreement exists on many critical points. What is presented here is probably the lowest common denominator on which most researchers would agree.

Organization of Information in Long-Term Memory

Physically, the brain consists of roughly 10 billion neurons, each analogous to a computer chip capable of storing information. Each neuron has octopus-like arms called axons and dendrites. Electrical impulses flow through these arms and are ferried by neurotransmitting chemicals across what is called the synaptic gap between neurons. Memories are stored as patterns of connections between neurons. When two neurons are activated, the connections or "synapses" between them are strengthened.

As you read this chapter, the experience actually causes physical changes in your brain. "In a matter of seconds, new circuits are formed that can change forever the way you think about the world."[30]

Memory records a lifetime of experience and thoughts. Such a massive data retrieval mechanism, like a library or computer system, must have an organizational structure; otherwise information that enters the system could never be retrieved. Imagine the Library of Congress if there were no indexing system.

There has been considerable research on how information is organized and represented in memory, but the findings remain speculative. Current research focuses on which sections of the brain process various types of information. This is determined by testing patients who have suffered brain damage from strokes and trauma or by using functional magnetic resonance imaging (fMRI) that "lights up" the active portion of the brain as a person speaks, reads, writes, or listens.

None of the current theories seems to encompass the full range or complexity of memory processes, which include memory for sights and sounds, for feelings, and for belief systems that integrate information on a large number of concepts. However useful the research has been for other purposes, analysts' needs are best served by a very simple image of the structure of memory.

Imagine memory as a massive, multidimensional spider web. This image captures what is, for the purposes of this book, perhaps the most important property of information stored in memory--its interconnectedness. One thought leads to another. It is possible to start at any one point in memory and follow a perhaps labyrinthine path to reach any other point. Information is retrieved by tracing through the network of interconnections to the place where it is stored.

Retrievability is influenced by the number of locations in which information is stored and the number and strength of pathways from this information to other concepts that might be activated by incoming information. The more frequently a path is followed, the stronger that path becomes and the more readily available the information located along that path. If one has not thought of a subject for some time, it may be difficult to recall details. After thinking our way back into the appropriate context and finding the general location in our memory, the interconnections become more readily available. We begin to remember names, places, and events that had seemed to be forgotten.

Once people have started thinking about a problem one way, the same mental circuits or pathways get activated and strengthened each time they think about it. This facilitates the retrieval of information. These same pathways, however, also become the mental ruts that make it difficult to reorganize the information mentally so as to see it from a different perspective. That explains why, in the previous chapter, once you saw the picture of the old woman it was difficult to see the young woman, or vice versa. A subsequent chapter will consider ways of breaking out of mental ruts.

One useful concept of memory organization is what some cognitive psychologists call a "schema." A schema is *any pattern of relationships* among data stored in memory. It is any set of nodes and links between them in the spider web of memory that hang together so strongly that they can be retrieved and used more or less as a single unit.

For example, a person may have a schema for a bar that when activated immediately makes available in memory knowledge of the properties of a bar and what distinguishes a bar, say, from a tavern. It brings back memories of specific bars that may in turn stimulate memories of thirst, guilt, or other feelings or circumstances. People also have schemata (plural for schema) for abstract concepts such as a socialist economic system and what distinguishes it from a capitalist or communist system. Schemata for phenomena such as success or failure in making an accurate intelligence estimate will include links to those elements of memory that explain typical causes and implications of success or failure. There must also be schemata for processes that link memories of the various steps involved in long division, regression analysis, or simply making inferences from evidence and writing an intelligence report.

Any given point in memory may be connected to many different overlapping schemata. This system is highly complex and not well understood.

This conception of a schema is so general that it begs many important questions of interest to memory researchers, but it is the best that can be done given the current state of knowledge. It serves the purpose of emphasizing that memory does have structure. It also shows that how knowledge is connected in memory is critically important in determining what information is retrieved in response to any stimulus and how that information is used in reasoning.

Concepts and schemata stored in memory exercise a powerful influence on the formation of perceptions from sensory data. Recall the experiment discussed in the previous chapter in which test subjects were exposed very briefly to playing cards that had been doctored so that some hearts were black and spades red. When retained in SIS for a fraction of a second, the spades were indeed red. In the course of interpreting the sensory impression and transferring it to STM, however, the spades became black because the memory system has no readily available schema for a red spade to be matched against the sensory impression. If information does not fit into what people know, or think they know, they have great difficulty processing it.

The content of schemata in memory is a principal factor distinguishing stronger from weaker analytical ability. This is aptly illustrated by an experiment with chess players. When chess grandmasters and masters and ordinary chess players were given five to 10 seconds to note the position of 20 to 25 chess pieces placed randomly on a chess board, the masters and ordinary players were alike in being able to remember the places of only about six pieces. If the positions of the pieces were taken from an actual game (unknown to the test subjects), however, the grandmasters and masters were usually able to reproduce almost all the positions without error, while the ordinary players were still able to place correctly only a half-dozen pieces.[31]

That the unique ability of the chess masters did not result from a pure feat of memory is indicated by the masters' inability to perform better than ordinary players in remembering randomly placed positions. Their exceptional performance in remembering positions from actual games stems from their ability to immediately perceive patterns that enable them to process many bits of information together as a single chunk or schema. The chess master has available in long-term memory many schemata that connect individual positions together in coherent patterns. When the position of chess pieces on the board corresponds to a recognized schema, it is very easy for the master to remember not only the positions of the pieces, but the outcomes of previous games in which the pieces were in these positions. Similarly, the unique abilities of the master analyst are attributable to the schemata in long-term memory that enable the analyst to perceive patterns in data that pass undetected by the average observer.

Getting Information Into and Out of Long-Term Memory

It used to be that how well a person learned something was thought to depend upon how long it was kept in short-term memory or the number of times they repeated it to themselves. Research evidence now suggests that neither of these factors plays the critical role. Continuous repetition does not necessarily guarantee that something will be remembered. The key factor in transferring information from short-term to long-term memory is the development of associations between the new information and schemata already available in memory. This, in turn, depends upon two variables: the extent to which the information to be learned relates to an already existing schema, and the level of processing given to the new information.

Take one minute to try to memorize the following items from a shopping list: bread, eggs, butter, salami, corn, lettuce, soap, jelly, chicken, and coffee. Chances are, you will try to burn the words into your mind by repeating them over and over. Such repetition, or maintenance rehearsal, is effective for maintaining the information in STM, but is an inefficient and often ineffective means of transferring it to LTM. The list is difficult to memorize because it does not correspond with any schema already in memory.

The words are familiar, but you do not have available in memory a schema that connects the words in this particular group to each other. If the list were changed to juice, cereal, milk, sugar, bacon, eggs, toast, butter, jelly, and coffee, the task would be much easier because the data would then correspond with an existing schema--items commonly eaten for breakfast. Such a list can be assimilated to your existing store of knowledge with little difficulty, just as the chess master rapidly assimilates the positions of many chessmen.

Depth of processing is the second important variable in determining how well information is retained. Depth of processing refers to the amount of effort and cognitive capacity employed to process information, and the number and strength of associations that are thereby forged between the data to be learned and knowledge already in memory. In experiments to test how well people remember a list of words, test subjects might be asked to perform different tasks that reflect different levels of processing. The following illustrative tasks are listed in order of the depth of mental processing required: say how many letters there are in each word on the list, give a word that rhymes with each word, make a mental image of each word, make up a story that incorporates each word.

It turns out that the greater the depth of processing, the greater the ability to recall words on a list. This result holds true regardless of whether the test subjects are informed in advance that the purpose of the experiment is to test them on their memory. Advising test subjects to expect a test makes almost no difference in their performance, presumably because it only leads them to rehearse the information in short-term memory, which is ineffective as compared with other forms of processing.

There are three ways in which information may be learned or committed to memory: by rote, assimilation, or use of a mnemonic device. Each of these procedures is discussed below.[32]

By Rote

Material to be learned is repeated verbally with sufficient frequency that it can later be repeated from memory without use of any memory aids. When information is learned by rote, it forms a separate schema not closely interwoven with previously held knowledge. That is, the mental processing adds little by way of elaboration to the new information, and the new information adds little to the elaboration of existing schemata. Learning by rote is a brute force technique. It seems to be the least efficient way of remembering.

By Assimilation

Information is learned by assimilation when the structure or substance of the information fits into some memory schema already possessed by the learner. The new information is assimilated to or linked to the existing schema and can be retrieved readily by first accessing the existing schema and then reconstructing the new information. Assimilation involves learning by comprehension and is, therefore, a desirable method, but it can only be used to learn information that is somehow related to our previous experience.

By Using a Mnemonic Device

A mnemonic device is any means of organizing or encoding information for the purpose of making it easier to remember. A high school student cramming for a geography test might use the acronym "HOMES" as a device for remembering the first letter of each of the Great Lakes--Huron, Ontario, etc.

To learn the first grocery list of disconnected words, you would create some structure for linking the words to each other and/or to information already in LTM. You might imagine yourself shopping or putting the items away and mentally picture where they are located on the shelves at the market or in the kitchen. Or you might imagine a story concerning one or more meals that include all these items. Any form of processing information in this manner is a more effective aid to retention than rote repetition. Even more effective systems for quickly memorizing lists of names or words have been devised by various memory experts, but these require some study and practice in their use.

Mnemonic devices are useful for remembering information that does not fit any appropriate conceptual structure or schema already in memory. They work by providing a simple, artificial structure to which the information to be learned is then linked. The mnemonic device supplies the mental "file categories" that ensure retrievability of information. To remember, first recall the mnemonic device, then access the desired information.

MEMORY AND INTELLIGENCE ANALYSIS

An analyst's memory provides continuous input into the analytical process. This input is of two types--additional factual information on historical background and context, and schemata the analyst uses to determine the meaning of newly acquired information. Information from memory may force itself on the analyst's awareness without any deliberate effort by the analyst to remember; or, recall of the information may require considerable time and strain. In either case, anything that influences what information is remembered or retrieved from memory also influences intelligence analysis.

Judgment is the joint product of the available information and what the analyst brings to the analysis of this information. An experiment documenting differences between chess masters and ordinary chess players was noted earlier. Similar research with medical doctors diagnosing illness indicates that differences between stronger and weaker performers are to be found in the organization of information and experience in long-term memory.[33] The same presumably holds true for intelligence analysts. Substantive knowledge and analytical experience determine the store of memories and schemata the analyst draws upon to generate and evaluate hypotheses. The key is not a simple ability to recall facts, but the ability to recall patterns that relate facts to each other and to broader concepts--and to employ procedures that facilitate this process.

Stretching the Limits of Working Memory

Limited information is available on what is commonly thought of as "working memory"--the collection of information that an analyst holds in the forefront of the mind as he or she does analysis. The general concept of working memory seems clear from personal introspection. In writing this chapter, I am very conscious of the constraints on my ability to keep many pieces of information in mind while experimenting with ways to organize this information and seeking words to express my thoughts. To help offset these limits on my working memory, I have accumulated a large number of written notes containing ideas and half-written paragraphs. Only by using such external memory aids am I able to cope with the volume and complexity of the information I want to use.

A well-known article written over 40 years ago, titled "The Magic Number Seven--Plus or Minus Two," contends that seven--plus or minus two--is the number of things people can keep in their head all at once. [34] That limitation on working memory is the source of many problems. People have difficulty grasping a problem in all its complexity. This is why we sometimes have trouble making up our minds. For example, we think first about the arguments in favor, and then about the arguments against, and we can't keep all those pros and cons in our head at the same time to get an overview of how they balance off against each other.

The recommended technique for coping with this limitation of working memory is called externalizing the problem--getting it out of one's head and down on paper in some simplified form that shows the main elements of the problem and how they relate to each other. Chapter 7, "Structuring Analytical Problems," discusses ways of doing this. They all involve breaking down a problem into its component parts and then preparing a simple "model" that shows how the parts relate to the whole. When working on a small part of the problem, the model keeps one from losing sight of the whole.

A simple model of an analytical problem facilitates the assimilation of new information into long-term memory; it provides a structure to which bits and pieces of information can be related. The model defines the categories for filing information in memory and retrieving it on demand. In other words, it serves as a mnemonic device that provides the hooks on which to hang information so that it can be found when needed.

The model is initially an artificial construct, like the previously noted acronym "HOMES." With usage, however, it rapidly becomes an integral part of one's conceptual structure--the set of schemata used in processing information. At this point, remembering new information occurs by assimilation rather than by mnemonics. This enhances the ability to recall and make inferences from a larger volume of information in a greater variety of ways than would otherwise be possible.

"Hardening of the Categories"

Memory processes tend to work with generalized categories. If people do not have an appropriate category for something, they are unlikely to perceive it, store it in memory, or be able to retrieve it from memory later. If categories are drawn incorrectly, people are likely to perceive and remember things inaccurately. When information about phenomena that are different in important respects nonetheless gets stored in memory under a single concept, errors of analysis may result. For example, many observers of international affairs had the impression that Communism was a monolithic movement, that it was the same everywhere and controlled from Moscow. All Communist countries were grouped together in a single, undifferentiated category called "international Communism" or "the Communist bloc." In 1948, this led many in the United States to downplay the importance of the Stalin-Tito split. According to one authority, it "may help explain why many Western minds, including scholars, remained relatively blind to the existence and significance of Sino-Soviet differences long after they had been made manifest in the realm of ideological formulae."[35]

"Hardening of the categories" is a common analytical weakness. Fine distinctions among categories and tolerance for ambiguity contribute to more effective analysis.

Things That Influence What Is Remembered

Factors that influence how information is stored in memory and that affect future retrievability include: being the first-stored information on a given topic, the amount of attention focused on the information, the credibility of the information, and the importance attributed to the information at the moment of storage. By influencing the content of memory, all of these factors also influence the outcome of intelligence analysis.

Chapter 12 on "Biases in Estimating Probabilities" describes how availability in memory influences judgments of probability. The more instances a person can recall of a phenomenon, the more probable that phenomenon seems to be. This is true even though ability to recall past examples is influenced by vividness of the information, how recently something occurred, its impact upon one's personal welfare, and many other factors unrelated to the actual probability of the phenomenon.

Memory Rarely Changes Retroactively

Analysts often receive new information that should, logically, cause them to reevaluate the credibility or significance of previous information. Ideally, the earlier information should then become either more salient and readily available in memory, or less so. But it does not work that way. Unfortunately, memories are seldom reassessed or reorganized retroactively in response to new information. For example, information that is dismissed as unimportant or irrelevant because it did not fit an analyst's expectations does not become more memorable even if the analyst changes his or her thinking to the point where the same information, received today, would be recognized as very significant.

Memory Can Handicap as Well as Help

Understanding how memory works provides some insight into the nature of creativity, openness to new information, and breaking mind-sets. All involve spinning new links in the spider web of memory--links among facts, concepts, and schemata that previously were not connected or only weakly connected.

Training courses for intelligence analysts sometimes focus on trying to open up an analyst's established mind-set, to get him or her to see problems from different perspectives in order to give a fairer shake to alternative explanations. More often than not, the reaction of experienced analysts is that they have devoted 20 years to developing their present mind-set, that it has served them well, and that they see no need to change it. Such analysts view themselves, often accurately, as comparable to the chess masters. They believe the information embedded in their long-term memory permits them to perceive patterns and make inferences that are beyond the reach of other observers. In one sense, they are quite correct in not wanting to change; it is, indeed, their existing schemata or mind-set that enables them to achieve whatever success they enjoy in making analytical judgments.

There is, however, a crucial difference between the chess master and the master intelligence analyst. Although the chess master faces a different opponent in each match, the environment in which each contest takes place remains stable and unchanging: the permissible moves of the diverse pieces are rigidly determined, and the rules cannot be changed without the master's knowledge. Once the chess master develops an accurate schema, there is no need to change it. The intelligence analyst, however, must cope with a rapidly changing world. Many countries that previously were US adversaries are now our formal or de facto allies. The American and Russian governments and societies are not the same today as they were 20 or even 10 or five years ago. Schemata that were valid yesterday may no longer be functional tomorrow.

Learning new schemata often requires the unlearning of existing ones, and this is exceedingly difficult. It is always easier to learn a new habit than to unlearn an old one. Schemata in long-term memory that are so essential to effective analysis are also the principal source of inertia in recognizing and adapting to a changing environment. Chapter 6, "Keeping an Open Mind," identifies tools for dealing with this problem.

PART II:
TOOLS FOR THINKING

Chapter 4

STRATEGIES FOR ANALYTICAL JUDGMENT: TRANSCENDING THE LIMITS OF INCOMPLETE INFORMATION

SUMMARY

When intelligence analysts make thoughtful analytical judgments, how do they do it? In seeking answers to this question, this chapter discusses the strengths and limitations of situational logic, theory, comparison, and simple immersion in the data as strategies for the generation and evaluation of hypotheses. The final section discusses alternative strategies for choosing among hypotheses. One strategy too often used by intelligence analysts is described as "satisficing"--choosing the first hypothesis that appears good enough rather than carefully identifying all possible hypotheses and determining which is most consistent with the evidence.[36]

Intelligence analysts should be self-conscious about their reasoning process. They should think about *how* they make judgments and reach conclusions, not just about the judgments and conclusions themselves. Webster's dictionary defines judgment as arriving at a "decision or conclusion on the basis of indications and probabilities when the facts are not clearly ascertained."[37] Judgment is what analysts use to fill gaps in their knowledge. It entails going beyond the available information and is the principal means of coping with uncertainty. It always involves an analytical leap, from the known into the uncertain.

Judgment is an integral part of all intelligence analysis. While the optimal goal of intelligence collection is complete knowledge, this goal is seldom reached in practice. Almost by definition of the intelligence mission, intelligence issues involve considerable uncertainty. Thus, the analyst is commonly working with incomplete, ambiguous, and often contradictory data. The intelligence analyst's function might be described as transcending the limits of incomplete information through the exercise of analytical judgment.

The ultimate nature of judgment remains a mystery. It is possible, however, to identify diverse strategies that analysts employ to process information as they prepare to pass judgment. Analytical strategies are important because they influence the data one attends to. They determine where the analyst shines his or her searchlight, and this inevitably affects the outcome of the analytical process.

STRATEGIES FOR GENERATING AND EVALUATING HYPOTHESES

This book uses the term hypothesis in its broadest sense as a potential explanation or conclusion that is to be tested by collecting and presenting evidence. Examination of how analysts generate and evaluate hypotheses identifies three principal strategies--the application of theory, situational logic, and comparison--each of which is discussed at some length below. A "non-strategy," immersion in the data and letting the data speak for themselves, is also discussed. This list of analytical strategies is not exhaustive. Other strategies might include, for example, projecting one's own psychological needs onto the data at hand, but this discussion is not concerned with the pathology of erroneous judgment. Rather, the goal is to understand the several kinds of careful, conscientious analysis one would hope and expect to find among a cadre of intelligence analysts dealing with highly complex issues.

Situational Logic

This is the most common operating mode for intelligence analysts. Generation and analysis of hypotheses start with consideration of concrete elements of the current situation, rather than with broad generalizations that encompass many similar cases. The situation is regarded as one-of-a-kind, so that it must be understood in terms of its own unique logic, rather than as one example of a broad class of comparable events.

Starting with the known facts of the current situation and an understanding of the unique forces at work at that particular time and place, the analyst seeks to identify the logical antecedents or consequences of this situation. A scenario is developed that hangs together as a plausible narrative. The analyst may work backwards to explain the origins or causes of the current situation or forward to estimate the future outcome.

Situational logic commonly focuses on tracing cause-effect relationships or, when dealing with purposive behavior, means-ends relationships. The analyst identifies the goals being pursued and explains why the foreign actor(s) believe certain means will achieve those goals.

Particular strengths of situational logic are its wide applicability and ability to integrate a large volume of relevant detail. Any situation, however unique, may be analyzed in this manner.

Situational logic as an analytical strategy also has two principal weaknesses. One is that it is so difficult to understand the mental and bureaucratic processes of foreign leaders and governments. To see the options faced by foreign leaders as these leaders see them, one must understand their values and assumptions and even their misperceptions and misunderstandings. Without such insight, interpreting foreign leaders' decisions or forecasting future decisions is often little more than partially informed speculation. Too frequently, foreign behavior appears "irrational" or "not in their own best interest." Such conclusions often indicate analysts have projected American values and conceptual frameworks onto the foreign leaders and societies, rather than understanding the logic of the situation as it appears to them.

The second weakness is that situational logic fails to exploit the theoretical knowledge derived from study of similar phenomena in other countries and other time periods. The subject of national separatist movements illustrates the point. Nationalism is a centuries-old problem, but most Western industrial democracies have been considered well-integrated national communities. Even so, recent years have seen an increase in pressures from minority ethnic groups seeking independence or autonomy. Why has this phenomenon occurred recently in Scotland, southern France and Corsica, Quebec, parts of Belgium, and Spain--as well as in less stable Third World countries where it might be expected?

Dealing with this topic in a logic-of-the-situation mode, a country analyst would examine the diverse political, economic, and social groups whose interests are at stake in the country. Based on the relative power positions of these groups, the dynamic interactions among them, and anticipated trends or developments that might affect the future positions of the interested parties, the analyst would seek to identify the driving forces that will determine the eventual outcome.

It is quite possible to write in this manner a detailed and seemingly well-informed study of a separatist movement in a single country while ignoring the fact that ethnic conflict as a generic phenomenon has been the subject of considerable theoretical study. By studying similar phenomena in many countries, one can generate and evaluate hypotheses concerning root causes that may not even be considered by an analyst who is dealing only with the logic of a single situation. For example, to what extent does the resurgence of long-dormant ethnic sentiments stem from a reaction against the cultural homogenization that accompanies modern mass communications systems?

Analyzing many examples of a similar phenomenon, as discussed below, enables one to probe more fundamental causes than those normally considered in logic-of-the-situation analysis. The proximate causes identified by situational logic appear, from the broader perspective of theoretical analysis, to be but symptoms indicating the presence of more fundamental causal factors. A better understanding of these fundamental causes is critical to effective forecasting, especially over the longer range. While situational logic may be the best approach to estimating short-term developments, a more theoretical approach is required as the analytical perspective moves further into the future.

Applying Theory

Theory is an academic term not much in vogue in the Intelligence Community, but it is unavoidable in any discussion of analytical judgment. In one popular meaning of the term, "theoretical" is associated with the terms "impractical" and "unrealistic". Needless to say, it is used here in a quite different sense.

A theory is a generalization based on the study of many examples of some phenomenon. It specifies that when a given set of conditions arises, certain other conditions will follow either with certainty or with some degree of probability. In other words, conclusions are judged to follow from a set of conditions and a finding that these conditions apply in the specific case being analyzed. For example, Turkey is a developing country in a precarious strategic position. This defines a set of conditions that imply conclusions concerning the role of the military and the nature of political processes in that country, because analysts have an implicit if not explicit understanding of how these factors normally relate.

What academics refer to as theory is really only a more explicit version of what intelligence analysts think of as their basic understanding of how individuals, institutions, and political systems normally behave.

There are both advantages and drawbacks to applying theory in intelligence analysis. One advantage is that "theory economizes thought." By identifying the key elements of a problem, theory enables an analyst to sort through a mass of less significant detail. Theory enables the analyst to see beyond today's transient developments, to recognize which trends are superficial and which are significant, and to foresee future developments for which there is today little concrete evidence.

Consider, for example, the theoretical proposition that economic development and massive infusion of foreign ideas in a feudal society lead to political instability. This proposition seems well established. When applied to Saudi Arabia, it suggests that the days of the Saudi monarchy are numbered, although analysts of the Saudi scene using situational logic find little or no current evidence of a meaningful threat to the power and position of the royal family. Thus, the application of a generally accepted theoretical proposition enables the analyst to forecast an outcome for which the "hard evidence" has not yet begun to develop. This is an important strength of theoretical analysis when applied to real-world problems.

Yet this same example also illustrates a common weakness in applying theory to analysis of political phenomena. Theoretical propositions frequently fail to specify the time frame within which developments might be anticipated to occur. The analytical problem with respect to Saudi Arabia is not so much whether the monarchy will *eventually* be replaced, as when or under what conditions this might happen. Further elaboration of the theory relating economic development and foreign ideas to political instability in feudal societies would identify early warning indicators that analysts might look for. Such indicators would guide both intelligence collection and analysis of sociopolitical and socioeconomic data and lead to hypotheses concerning when or under what circumstances such an event might occur.

But if theory enables the analyst to transcend the limits of available data, it may also provide the basis for ignoring evidence that is truly indicative of future events. Consider the following theoretical propositions in the light of popular agitation against the Shah of Iran in the late 1970s: (1) When the position of an authoritarian ruler is threatened, he will defend his position with force if necessary. (2) An authoritarian ruler enjoying complete support of effective military and security forces cannot be overthrown by popular opinion and agitation. Few would challenge these propositions, yet when applied to Iran in the late 1970s, they led Iran specialists to misjudge the Shah's chances for retaining the peacock throne. Many if not most such specialists seemed convinced that the Shah remained strong and that he would crack down on dissent when it threatened to get out of control. Many persisted in this assessment for several months after the accumulation of what in retrospect appears to have been strong evidence to the contrary.

Persistence of these assumptions is easily understood in psychological terms. When evidence is lacking or ambiguous, the analyst evaluates hypotheses by applying his or her general background knowledge concerning the nature of political systems and behavior. The evidence on the strength of the Shah and his intention to crack down on dissidents was ambiguous, but the Iranian monarch was an authoritarian ruler, and authoritarian regimes were assumed to have certain characteristics, as noted in the previously cited propositions. Thus beliefs about the Shah were embedded in broad and persuasive assumptions about the nature of authoritarian regimes *per se*. For an analyst who believed in the two aforementioned propositions, it would have taken far more evidence, including more unambiguous evidence, to infer that the Shah would be overthrown than to justify continued confidence in his future.[38]

Figure 4 below illustrates graphically the difference between theory and situational logic. Situational logic looks at the evidence within a single country on multiple interrelated issues, as shown by the column highlighted in gray. This is a typical area studies approach. Theoretical analysis looks at the evidence related to a single issue in multiple countries, as shown by the row highlighted in gray. This is a typical social science approach.

	Country	Country	Country	Country
Issue	Evidence	Evidence	Evidence	Evidence
Issue	Evidence	Evidence	Evidence	Evidence
Issue	Evidence	Evidence	Evidence	Evidence
Issue	Evidence	Evidence	Evidence	Evidence

Figure 4 Situational Logic vs. Theory

The distinction between theory and situational logic is not as clear as it may seem from this graphic, however. Logic-of-the-situation analysis also draws heavily on theoretical assumptions. How does the analyst select the most significant elements to describe the current situation, or identify the causes or consequences of these elements, without some implicit theory that relates the likelihood of certain outcomes to certain antecedent conditions?

For example, if the analyst estimating the outcome of an impending election does not have current polling data, it is necessary to look back at past elections, study the campaigns, and then judge how voters are likely to react to the current campaigns and to events that influence voter attitudes. In doing so, the analyst operates from a set of assumptions about human nature and what drives people and groups. These assumptions form part of a theory of political behavior, but it is a different sort of theory than was discussed under theoretical analysis. It does not illuminate the entire situation, but only a small increment of the situation, and it may not apply beyond the specific country of concern. Further, it is much more likely to remain implicit, rather than be a focal point of the analysis.

Comparison with Historical Situations

A third approach for going beyond the available information is comparison. An analyst seeks understanding of current events by comparing them with historical precedents in the same country, or with similar events in other countries. Analogy is one form of comparison. When an historical situation is deemed comparable to current circumstances, analysts use their understanding of the historical precedent to fill gaps in their understanding of the current situation. Unknown elements of the present are assumed to be the same as known elements of the historical precedent. Thus, analysts reason that the same forces are at work, that the outcome of the present situation is likely to be similar to the outcome of the historical situation, or that a certain policy is required in order to avoid the same outcome as in the past.

Comparison differs from situational logic in that the present situation is interpreted in the light of a more or less explicit conceptual model that is created by looking at similar situations in other times or places. It differs from theoretical analysis in that this conceptual model is based on a single case or only a few cases, rather than on many similar cases. Comparison may also be used to generate theory, but this is a more narrow kind of theorizing that cannot be validated nearly as well as generalizations inferred from many comparable cases.

Reasoning by comparison is a convenient shortcut, one chosen when neither data nor theory are available for the other analytical strategies, or simply because it is easier and less time-consuming than a more detailed analysis. A careful comparative analysis starts by specifying key elements of the present situation. The analyst then seeks out one or more historical precedents that may shed light on the present. Frequently, however, a historical precedent may be so vivid and powerful that it imposes itself upon a person's thinking from the outset, conditioning them to perceive the present primarily in terms of its similarity to the past. This is reasoning by analogy. As Robert Jervis noted, "historical analogies often precede, rather than follow, a careful analysis of a situation."[39]

The tendency to relate contemporary events to earlier events as a guide to understanding is a powerful one. Comparison helps achieve understanding by reducing the unfamiliar to the familiar. In the absence of data required for a full understanding of the current situation, reasoning by comparison may be the only alternative. Anyone taking this approach, however, should be aware of the significant potential for error. This course is an implicit admission of the lack of sufficient information to understand the present situation in its own right, and lack of relevant theory to relate the present situation to many other comparable situations

The difficulty, of course, is in being certain that two situations are truly comparable. Because they are equivalent in some respects, there is a tendency to reason as though they were equivalent in all respects, and to assume that the current situation will have the same or similar outcome as the historical situation. This is a valid assumption only when based on in-depth analysis of both the current situation *and* the historical precedent to ensure that they are actually comparable in all relevant respects.

In a short book that ought to be familiar to all intelligence analysts, Ernest May traced the impact of historical analogy on US foreign policy.[40] He found that because of reasoning by analogy, US policymakers tend to be one generation behind, determined to avoid the mistakes of the previous generation. They pursue the policies that would have been most appropriate in the historical situation but are not necessarily well adapted to the current one.

Policymakers in the 1930s, for instance, viewed the international situation as analogous to that before World War I. Consequently, they followed a policy of isolation that would have been appropriate for preventing American involvement in the first World War but failed to prevent the second. Communist aggression after World War II was seen as analogous to Nazi aggression, leading to a policy of containment that could have prevented World War II.

More recently, the Vietnam analogy has been used repeatedly over many years to argue against an activist US foreign policy. For example, some used the Vietnam analogy to argue against US participation in the Gulf War--a flawed analogy because the operating terrain over which battles were fought was completely different in Kuwait/Iraq and much more in our favor there as compared with Vietnam.

May argues that policymakers often perceive problems in terms of analogies with the past, but that they ordinarily use history badly:

> When resorting to an analogy, they tend to seize upon the first that comes to mind. They do not research more widely. Nor do they pause to analyze the case, test its fitness, or even ask in what ways it might be misleading.[41]

As compared with policymakers, intelligence analysts have more time available to "analyze rather than analogize." Intelligence analysts tend to be good historians, with a large number of historical precedents available for recall. The greater the number of potential analogues an analyst has at his or her disposal, the greater the likelihood of selecting an appropriate one. The greater the depth of an analyst's knowledge, the greater the chances the analyst will perceive the differences as well as the similarities between two situations. Even under the best of circumstances, however, inferences based on comparison with a single analogous situation probably are more prone to error than most other forms of inference.

The most productive uses of comparative analysis are to suggest hypotheses and to highlight differences, not to draw conclusions. Comparison can suggest the presence or the influence of variables that are not readily apparent in the current situation, or stimulate the imagination to conceive explanations or possible outcomes that might not otherwise occur to the analyst. In short, comparison can generate hypotheses that then guide the search for additional information to confirm or refute these hypotheses. It should not, however, form the basis for conclusions unless thorough analysis of both situations has confirmed they are indeed comparable.

Data Immersion

Analysts sometimes describe their work procedure as immersing themselves in the data without fitting the data into any preconceived pattern. At some point an apparent pattern (or answer or explanation) emerges spontaneously, and the analyst then goes back to the data to check how well the data support this judgment. According to this view, objectivity requires the analyst to suppress any personal opinions or preconceptions, so as to be guided only by the "facts" of the case.

To think of analysis in this way overlooks the fact that information cannot speak for itself. The significance of information is always a joint function of the nature of the information and the context in which it is interpreted. The context is provided by the analyst in the form of a set of assumptions and expectations concerning human and organizational behavior. These preconceptions are critical determinants of which information is considered relevant and how it is interpreted.

Of course there are many circumstances in which the analyst has no option but to immerse himself or herself in the data. Obviously, an analyst must have a base of knowledge to work with before starting analysis. When dealing with a new and unfamiliar subject, the uncritical and relatively non-selective accumulation and review of information is an appropriate first step. But this is a process of absorbing information, not analyzing it.

Analysis begins when the analyst consciously inserts himself or herself into the process to select, sort, and organize information. This selection and organization can only be accomplished according to conscious or subconscious assumptions and preconceptions.

The question is not whether one's prior assumptions and expectations influence analysis, but only whether this influence is made explicit or remains implicit. The distinction appears to be important. In research to determine how physicians make medical diagnoses, the doctors who comprised the test subjects were asked to describe their analytical strategies. Those who stressed thorough collection of data as their principal analytical method were significantly less accurate in their diagnoses than those who described themselves as following other analytical strategies such as identifying and testing hypotheses.[42] Moreover, the collection of additional data through greater thoroughness in the medical history and physical examination did not lead to increased diagnostic accuracy.[43]

One might speculate that the analyst who seeks greater objectivity by suppressing recognition of his or her own subjective input actually has less valid input to make. Objectivity is gained by making assumptions explicit so that they may be examined and challenged, not by vain efforts to eliminate them from analysis.

RELATIONSHIPS AMONG STRATEGIES

No one strategy is necessarily better than the others. In order to generate all relevant hypotheses and make maximum use of all potentially relevant information, it would be desirable to employ all three strategies at the early hypothesis generation phase of a research project. Unfortunately, analysts commonly lack the inclination or time to do so.

Different analysts have different analytical habits and preferences for analytical strategy. As a broad generalization that admits numerous exceptions, analysts trained in area studies or history tend to prefer situational logic, while those with a strong social science background are more likely to bring theoretical and comparative insights to bear on their work. The Intelligence Community as a whole is far stronger in situational logic than in theory. In my judgment, intelligence analysts do not generalize enough, as opposed to many academic scholars who generalize too much. This is especially true in political analysis, and it is not entirely due to unavailability of applicable political theory. Theoretical insights that are available are often unknown to or at least not used by political intelligence analysts.

Differences in analytical strategy may cause fundamental differences in perspective between intelligence analysts and some of the policymakers for whom they write. Higher level officials who are not experts on the subject at issue use far more theory and comparison and less situational logic than intelligence analysts. Any policymaker or other senior manager who lacks the knowledge base of the specialist and does not have time for detail must, of necessity, deal with broad generalizations. Many decisions must be made, with much less time to consider each of them than is available to the intelligence analyst. This requires the policymaker to take a more conceptual approach, to think in terms of theories, models, or analogies that summarize large amounts of detail. Whether this represents sophistication or oversimplification depends upon the individual case and, perhaps, whether one agrees or disagrees with the judgments made. In any event, intelligence analysts would do well to take this phenomenon into account when writing for their consumers.

STRATEGIES FOR CHOICE AMONG HYPOTHESES

A systematic analytical process requires selection among alternative hypotheses, and it is here that analytical practice often diverges significantly from the ideal and from the canons of scientific method. The ideal is to generate a full set of hypotheses, systematically evaluate each hypothesis, and then identify the hypothesis that provides the best fit to the data. Scientific method, for its part, requires that one seek to disprove hypotheses rather than confirm them.

In practice, other strategies are commonly employed. Alexander George has identified a number of less-than-optimal strategies for making decisions in the face of incomplete information and multiple, competing values and goals. While George conceived of these strategies as applicable to how decisionmakers choose among alternative policies, most also apply to how intelligence analysts might decide among alternative analytical hypotheses.

The relevant strategies George identified are:

- "Satisficing"--selecting the first identified alternative that appears "good enough" rather than examining all alternatives to determine which is "best."
- Incrementalism--focusing on a narrow range of alternatives representing marginal change, without considering the need for dramatic change from an existing position.
- Consensus--opting for the alternative that will elicit the greatest agreement and support. Simply telling the boss what he or she wants to hear is one version of this.
- Reasoning by analogy--choosing the alternative that appears most likely to avoid some previous error or to duplicate a previous success.
- Relying on a set of principles or maxims that distinguish a "good" from a "bad" alternative.[44]

The intelligence analyst has another tempting option not available to the policymaker: to avoid judgment by simply describing the current situation, identifying alternatives, and letting the intelligence consumer make the judgment about which alternative is most likely. Most of these strategies are not discussed here. The following paragraphs focus only on the one that seems most prevalent in intelligence analysis.

"Satisficing"

I would suggest, based on personal experience and discussions with analysts, that most analysis is conducted in a manner very similar to the satisficing mode (selecting the first identified alternative that appears "good enough").[45] The analyst identifies what appears to be the most likely hypothesis--that is, the tentative estimate, explanation, or description of the situation that appears most accurate. Data are collected and organized according to whether they support this tentative judgment, and the hypothesis is accepted if it seems to provide a reasonable fit to the data. The careful analyst will then make a quick review of other possible hypotheses and of evidence not accounted for by the preferred judgment to ensure that he or she has not overlooked some important consideration.

This approach has three weaknesses: the selective perception that results from focus on a single hypothesis, failure to generate a complete set of competing hypotheses, and a focus on evidence that confirms rather than disconfirms hypotheses. Each of these is discussed below.

Selective Perception

Tentative hypotheses serve a useful function in helping analysts select, organize, and manage information. They narrow the scope of the problem so that the analyst can focus efficiently on data that are most relevant and important. The hypotheses serve as organizing frameworks in working memory and thus facilitate retrieval of information from memory. In short, they are essential elements of the analytical process. But their functional utility also entails some cost, because a hypothesis functions as a perceptual filter. Analysts, like people in general, tend to see what they are looking for and to overlook that which is not specifically included in their search strategy. They tend to limit the processed information to that which is relevant to the current hypothesis. If the hypothesis is incorrect, information may be lost that would suggest a new or modified hypothesis.

This difficulty can be overcome by the simultaneous consideration of multiple hypotheses. This approach is discussed in detail in Chapter 8. It has the advantage of focusing attention on those few items of evidence that have the greatest diagnostic value in distinguishing among the validity of competing hypotheses. Most evidence is consistent with several different hypotheses, and this fact is easily overlooked when analysts focus on only one hypothesis at a time--especially if their focus is on seeking to confirm rather than disprove what appears to be the most likely answer.

Failure to Generate Appropriate Hypotheses

If tentative hypotheses determine the criteria for searching for information and judging its relevance, it follows that one may overlook the proper answer if it is not encompassed within the several hypotheses being considered. Research on hypothesis generation suggests that performance on this task is woefully inadequate.[46]When faced with an analytical problem, people are either unable or simply do not take the time to identify the full range of potential answers. Analytical performance might be significantly enhanced by more deliberate attention to this stage of the analytical process. Analysts need to take more time to develop a full set of competing hypotheses, using all three of the previously discussed strategies--theory, situational logic, and comparison.

Failure to Consider Diagnosticity of Evidence

In the absence of a complete set of alternative hypotheses, it is not possible to evaluate the "diagnosticity" of evidence. Unfortunately, many analysts are unfamiliar with the concept of diagnosticity of evidence. It refers to the extent to which any item of evidence helps the analyst determine the relative likelihood of alternative hypotheses.

To illustrate, a high temperature may have great value in telling a doctor that a patient is sick, but relatively little value in determining which illness the patient is suffering from. Because a high temperature is consistent with so many possible hypotheses about a patient's illness, it has limited diagnostic value in determining which illness (hypothesis) is the more likely one.

Evidence is diagnostic when it influences an analyst's judgment on the *relative* likelihood of the various hypotheses. If an item of evidence seems consistent with all the hypotheses, it may have no diagnostic value at all. It is a common experience to discover that most available evidence really is not very helpful, as it can be reconciled with all the hypotheses.

Failure to Reject Hypotheses

Scientific method is based on the principle of rejecting hypotheses, while tentatively accepting only those hypotheses that cannot be refuted. Intuitive analysis, by comparison, generally concentrates on confirming a hypothesis and commonly accords more weight to evidence supporting a hypothesis than to evidence that weakens it. Ideally, the reverse would be true. While analysts usually cannot apply the statistical procedures of scientific methodology to test their hypotheses, they can and should adopt the conceptual strategy of seeking to refute rather than confirm hypotheses.

There are two aspects to this problem: people do not naturally seek disconfirming evidence, and when such evidence is received it tends to be discounted. If there is any question about the former, consider how often people test their political and religious beliefs by reading newspapers and books representing an opposing viewpoint. Concerning the latter, we have noted in Chapter 2, "Perception: Why Can't We See What Is There to Be Seen?" the tendency to accommodate new information to existing images. This is easy to do if information supporting a hypothesis is accepted as valid, while information that weakens it is judged to be of questionable reliability or an unimportant anomaly. When information is processed in this manner, it is easy to "confirm" almost any hypothesis that one already believes to be true.

Apart from the psychological pitfalls involved in seeking confirmatory evidence, an important logical point also needs to be considered. The logical reasoning underlying the scientific method of rejecting hypotheses is that "...no confirming instance of a law is a verifying instance, but that any disconfirming instance is a falsifying instance."[47] In other words, a hypothesis can never be proved by the enumeration of even a large body of evidence consistent with that hypothesis, because the same body of evidence may also be consistent with other hypotheses. A hypothesis may be disproved, however, by citing a single item of evidence that is incompatible with it.

P. C. Wason conducted a series of experiments to test the view that people generally seek confirming rather than disconfirming evidence.[48] The experimental design was based on the above point that the validity of a hypothesis can only be tested by seeking to disprove it rather than confirm it. Test subjects were given the three-number sequence, 2 - 4 - 6, and asked to discover the rule employed to generate this sequence. In order to do so, they were permitted to generate three-number sequences of their own and to ask the experimenter whether these conform to the rule. They were encouraged to generate and ask about as many sequences as they wished and were instructed to stop only when they believed they had discovered the rule.

There are, of course, many possible rules that might account for the sequence 2 - 4 - 6. The test subjects formulated tentative hypotheses such as any ascending sequence of even numbers, or any sequence separated by two digits. As expected, the test subjects generally took the incorrect approach of trying to confirm rather than eliminate such hypotheses. To test the hypothesis that the rule was any ascending sequence of even numbers, for example, they might ask if the sequence 8 - 10 - 14 conforms to the rule.

Readers who have followed the reasoning to this point will recognize that this hypothesis can never be proved by enumerating examples of ascending sequences of even numbers that are found to conform to the sought-for rule. One can only disprove the hypothesis by citing an ascending sequence of odd numbers and learning that this, too, conforms to the rule.

The correct rule was any three ascending numbers, either odd or even. Because of their strategy of seeking confirming evidence, only six of the 29 test subjects in Wason's experiment were correct the first time they thought they had discovered the rule. When this same experiment was repeated by a different researcher for a somewhat different purpose, none of the 51 test subjects had the right answer the first time they thought they had discovered the rule.[49]

In the Wason experiment, the strategy of seeking confirming rather than disconfirming evidence was particularly misleading because the 2 - 4 - 6 sequence is consistent with such a large number of hypotheses. It was easy for test subjects to obtain confirmatory evidence for almost any hypothesis they tried to confirm. It is important to recognize that comparable situations, when evidence is consistent with several different hypotheses, are extremely common in intelligence analysis.

Consider lists of early warning indicators, for example. They are designed to be indicative of an impending attack. Very many of them, however, are also consistent with the hypothesis that military movements are a bluff to exert diplomatic pressure and that no military action will be forthcoming. When analysts seize upon only one of these hypotheses and seek evidence to confirm it, they will often be led astray.

The evidence available to the intelligence analyst is in one important sense different from the evidence available to test subjects asked to infer the number sequence rule. The intelligence analyst commonly deals with problems in which the evidence has only a probabilistic relationship to the hypotheses being considered. Thus it is seldom possible to eliminate any hypothesis entirely, because the most one can say is that a given hypothesis is unlikely given the nature of the evidence, not that it is impossible.

This weakens the conclusions that can be drawn from a strategy aimed at eliminating hypotheses, but it does not in any way justify a strategy aimed at confirming them.

Circumstances and insufficient data often preclude the application of rigorous scientific procedures in intelligence analysis--including, in particular, statistical methods for testing hypotheses. There is, however, certainly no reason why the basic conceptual strategy of looking for contrary evidence cannot be employed. An optimal analytical strategy requires that analysts search for information to disconfirm their favorite theories, not employ a satisficing strategy that permits acceptance of the first hypothesis that seems consistent with the evidence.

CONCLUSION

There are many detailed assessments of intelligence failures, but few comparable descriptions of intelligence successes. In reviewing the literature on intelligence successes, Frank Stech found many examples of success but only three accounts that provide sufficient methodological details to shed light on the intellectual processes and methods that contributed to the successes. These dealt with successful American and British intelligence efforts during World War II to analyze German propaganda, predict German submarine movements, and estimate future capabilities and intentions of the German Air Force.[50]

Stech notes that in each of these highly successful efforts, the analysts employed procedures that "... facilitated the formulation and testing against each other of alternative hypothetical estimates of enemy intentions. Each of the three accounts stressed this pitting of competing hypotheses against the evidence."[51]

The simultaneous evaluation of multiple, competing hypotheses permits a more systematic and objective analysis than is possible when an analyst focuses on a single, most-likely explanation or estimate. The simultaneous evaluation of multiple, competing hypotheses entails far greater cognitive strain than examining a single, most-likely hypothesis. Retaining multiple hypotheses in working memory and noting how each item of evidence fits into each hypothesis add up to a formidable cognitive task. That is why this approach is seldom employed in intuitive analysis of complex issues. It can be accomplished, however, with the help of simple procedures described in Chapter 8, "Analysis of Competing Hypotheses."

Chapter 5

DO YOU REALLY NEED MORE INFORMATION?

SUMMARY

The difficulties associated with intelligence analysis are often attributed to the inadequacy of available information. Thus the US Intelligence Community invests heavily in improved intelligence collection systems while managers of analysis lament the comparatively small sums devoted to enhancing analytical resources, improving analytical methods, or gaining better understanding of the cognitive processes involved in making analytical judgments. This chapter questions the often-implicit assumption that lack of information is the principal obstacle to accurate intelligence judgments.[52]

Using experts in a variety of fields as test subjects, experimental psychologists have examined the relationship between the amount of information available to the experts, the accuracy of judgments they make based on this information, and the experts' confidence in the accuracy of these judgments. The word "information," as used in this context, refers to the totality of material an analyst has available to work with in making a judgment.

Using experts in a variety of fields as test subjects, experimental psychologists have examined the relationship between the amount of information available to the experts, the accuracy of judgments they make based on this information, and the experts' confidence in the accuracy of these judgments. The word "information," as used in this context, refers to the totality of material an analyst has available to work with in making a judgment.

Key findings from this research are:

- Once an experienced analyst has the minimum information necessary to make an informed judgment, obtaining additional information generally does not improve the accuracy of his or her estimates. Additional information does, however, lead the analyst to become more confident in the judgment, to the point of overconfidence.

- Experienced analysts have an imperfect understanding of what information they actually use in making judgments. They are unaware of the extent to which their judgments are determined by a few dominant factors, rather than by the systematic integration of all available information. Analysts actually use much less of the available information than they think they do.

As will be noted below, these experimental findings should not necessarily be accepted at face value. For example, circumstances exist in which additional information does contribute to more accurate analysis. However, there also are circumstances in which additional information-- particularly contradictory information--decreases rather than increases an analyst's confidence.

To interpret the disturbing but not surprising findings from these experiments, it is necessary to consider four different types of information and discuss their relative value in contributing to the accuracy of analytical judgments. It is also helpful to distinguish analysis in which results are driven by the data from analysis that is driven by the conceptual framework employed to interpret the data.

Understanding the complex relationship between amount of information and accuracy of judgment has implications for both the management and conduct of intelligence analysis. Such an understanding suggests analytical procedures and management initiatives that may indeed contribute to more accurate analytical judgments. It also suggests that resources needed to attain a better understanding of the entire analytical process might profitably be diverted from some of the more costly intelligence collection programs.

These findings have broad relevance beyond the Intelligence Community. Analysis of information to gain a better understanding of current developments and to estimate future outcomes is an essential component of decisionmaking in any field. In fact, the psychological experiments that are most relevant have been conducted with experts in such diverse fields as medical and psychological diagnosis, stock market analysis, weather forecasting, and horserace handicapping. The experiments reflect basic human processes that affect analysis of any subject.

One may conduct experiments to demonstrate these phenomena in any field in which experts analyze a finite number of identifiable and classifiable kinds of information to make judgments or estimates that can subsequently be checked for accuracy. The stock market analyst, for example, commonly works with information concerning price-earnings ratios, profit margins, earnings per share, market volume, and resistance and support levels, and it is relatively easy to measure quantitatively the accuracy of the resulting predictions. By controlling the information made available to a group of experts and then checking the accuracy of judgments based on this information, it is possible to investigate how people use information to arrive at analytical judgments.

AN EXPERIMENT: BETTING ON THE HORSES

A description of one such experiment serves to illustrate the procedure.[53] Eight experienced horserace handicappers were shown a list of 88 variables found on a typical past-performance chart--for example, the weight to be carried; the percentage of races in which horse finished first, second, or third during the previous year; the jockey's record; and the number of days since the horse's last race. Each handicapper was asked to identify, first, what he considered to be the five most important items of information--those he would wish to use to handicap a race if he were limited to only five items of information per horse. Each was then asked to select the 10, 20, and 40 most important variables he would use if limited to those levels of information.

At this point, the handicappers were given true data (sterilized so that horses and actual races could not be identified) for 40 past races and were asked to rank the top five horses in each race in order of expected finish. Each handicapper was given the data in increments of the 5, 10, 20 and 40 variables he had judged to be most useful. Thus, he predicted each race four times--once with each of the four different levels of information. For each prediction, each handicapper assigned a value from 0 to 100 percent to indicate degree of confidence in the accuracy of his prediction.

When the handicappers' predictions were compared with the actual outcomes of these 40 races, it was clear that average accuracy of predictions remained the same regardless of how much information the handicappers had available. Three of the handicappers actually showed less accuracy as the amount of information increased, two improved their accuracy, and three were unchanged. All, however, expressed steadily increasing confidence in their judgments as more information was received. This relationship between amount of information, accuracy of the handicappers' prediction of the first place winners, and the handicappers' confidence in their predictions is shown in Figure 5.

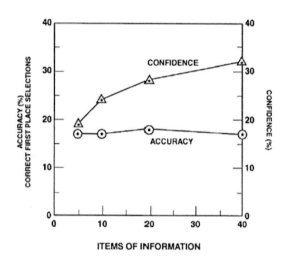

Figure 5 Items of information

With only five items of information, the handicappers' confidence was well calibrated with their accuracy, but they became overconfident as additional information was received.

The same relationships among amount of information, accuracy, and analyst confidence have been confirmed by similar experiments in other fields.[54] In one experiment with clinical psychologists, a psychological case file was divided into four sections representing successive chronological periods in the life of a relatively normal individual. Thirty-two psychologists with varying levels of experience were asked to make judgments on the basis of this information. After reading each section of the case file, the psychologists answered 25 questions (for which there were known answers) about the personality of the subject of the file. As in other experiments, increasing information resulted in a strong rise in confidence but a negligible increase in accuracy.[55]

A series of experiments to examine the mental processes of medical doctors diagnosing illness found little relationship between thoroughness of data collection and accuracy of diagnosis. Medical students whose self-described research strategy stressed thorough collection of information (as opposed to formation and testing of hypotheses) were significantly below average in the accuracy of their diagnoses. It seems that the explicit formulation of hypotheses directs a more efficient and effective search for information.[56]

MODELING EXPERT JUDGMENT

Another significant question concerns the extent to which analysts possess an accurate understanding of their own mental processes. How good is their insight into how they actually weight evidence in making judgments? For each situation to be analyzed, they have an implicit "mental model" consisting of beliefs and assumptions as to which variables are most important and how they are related to each other. If analysts have good insight into their own mental model, they should be able to identify and describe the variables they have considered most important in making judgments.

There is strong experimental evidence, however, that such self-insight is usually faulty. The expert perceives his or her own judgmental process, including the number of different kinds of information taken into account, as being considerably more complex than is in fact the case. Experts overestimate the importance of factors that have only a minor impact on their judgment and underestimate the extent to which their decisions are based on a few major variables. In short, people's mental models are simpler than they think, and the analyst is typically unaware not only of which variables *should* have the greatest influence, but also which variables *actually* are having the greatest influence.

All this has been demonstrated by experiments in which analysts were asked to make quantitative estimates concerning a relatively large number of cases in their area of expertise, with each case defined by a number of quantifiable factors. In one experiment, for example, stock market analysts were asked to predict long-term price appreciation for 50 securities, with each security being described in such terms as price/earnings ratio, corporate earnings growth trend, and dividend yield.[57] After completing this task, the analysts were asked to explain how they reached their conclusions, including how much weight they attached to each of the variables. They were instructed to be sufficiently explicit that another person going through the same information could apply the same judgmental rules and arrive at the same conclusions.

In order to compare this verbal rationalization with the judgmental policy reflected in the stock market analysts' actual decisions, multiple regression analysis or other similar statistical procedures can be used to develop a mathematical model of how each analyst actually weighed and combined information on the relevant variables.[58] There have been at least eight studies of this type in diverse fields,[59] including one involving prediction of future socioeconomic growth of underdeveloped nations.[60] The mathematical model based on the analyst's actual decisions is invariably a more accurate description of that analyst's decisionmaking than the analyst's own verbal description of how the judgments were made.

Although the existence of this phenomenon has been amply demonstrated, its causes are not well understood. The literature on these experiments contains only the following speculative explanation:

> Possibly our feeling that we can take into account a host of different factors comes about because, although we remember that at some time or other we have attended to each of the different factors, we fail to notice that it is seldom more than one or two that we consider at any one time.[61]

When Does New Information Affect Our Judgment?

To evaluate the relevance and significance of these experimental findings in the context of intelligence analysts' experiences, it is necessary to distinguish four types of additional information that an analyst might receive:

- **Additional detail about variables already included in the analysis:** Much raw intelligence reporting falls into this category. One would not expect such supplementary information to affect the overall accuracy of the analyst's judgment, and it is readily understandable that further detail that is consistent with previous information increases the analyst's confidence. Analyses for which considerable depth of detail is available to support the conclusions tend to be more persuasive to their authors as well as to their readers.

- **Identification of additional variables:** Information on additional variables permits the analyst to take into account other factors that may affect the situation. This is the kind of additional information used in the horserace handicapper experiment. Other experiments have employed some combination of additional variables and additional detail on the same variables. The finding that judgments are based on a few critical variables rather than on the entire spectrum of evidence helps to explain why information on additional variables does not normally improve predictive accuracy. Occasionally, in situations when there are known gaps in an analyst's understanding, a single report concerning some new and previously unconsidered factor--for example, an authoritative report on a policy decision or planned coup d'etat--will have a major impact on the analyst's judgment. Such a report would fall into one of the next two categories of new information.

- **Information concerning the value attributed to variables already included in the analysis:** An example of such information would be the horserace handicapper learning that a horse he thought would carry 110 pounds will actually carry only 106. Current intelligence reporting tends to deal with this kind of information; for example, an analyst may learn that a dissident group is stronger than had been anticipated. New facts affect the accuracy of judgments when they deal with changes in variables that are critical to the estimates. Analysts' confidence in judgments based on such information is influenced by their confidence in the accuracy of the information as well as by the amount of information.

- **Information concerning which variables are most important and how they relate to each other:** Knowledge and assumptions as to which variables are most important and how they are interrelated comprise the mental model that tells the analyst how to analyze the data received. Explicit investigation of such relationships is one factor that distinguishes systematic research from current intelligence reporting and raw intelligence. In the context of the horserace handicapper experiment, for example, handicappers had to select which variables to include in their analysis. Is weight carried by a horse more, or less, important than several other variables that affect a horse's performance? Any information that affects this judgment influences how the handicapper analyzes the available data; that is, it affects his mental model.

The accuracy of an analyst's judgment depends upon both the accuracy of our mental model (the fourth type of information discussed above) and the accuracy of the values attributed to the key variables in the model (the third type of information discussed above). Additional detail on variables already in the analyst's mental model and information on other variables that do not in fact have a significant influence on our judgment (the first and second types of information) have a negligible impact on accuracy, but form the bulk of the raw material analysts work with. These kinds of information increase confidence because the conclusions seem to be supported by such a large body of data.

This discussion of types of new information is the basis for distinguishing two types of analysis- data-driven analysis and conceptually-driven analysis.

Data-Driven Analysis

In this type of analysis, accuracy depends primarily upon the accuracy and completeness of the available data. If one makes the reasonable assumption that the analytical model is correct and the further assumption that the analyst properly applies this model to the data, then the accuracy of the analytical judgment depends entirely upon the accuracy and completeness of the data.

Analyzing the combat readiness of a military division is an example of data-driven analysis. In analyzing combat readiness, the rules and procedures to be followed are relatively well established. The totality of these procedures comprises a mental model that influences perception of the intelligence collected on the unit and guides judgment concerning what information is important and how this information should be analyzed to arrive at judgments concerning readiness.

Most elements of the mental model can be made explicit so that other analysts may be taught to understand and follow the same analytical procedures and arrive at the same or similar results. There is broad, though not necessarily universal, agreement on what the appropriate model is. There are relatively objective standards for judging the quality of analysis, inasmuch as the conclusions follow logically from the application of the agreed-upon model to the available data.

Conceptually Driven Analysis

Conceptually driven analysis is at the opposite end of the spectrum from data-driven analysis. The questions to be answered do not have neat boundaries, and there are many unknowns. The number of potentially relevant variables and the diverse and imperfectly understood relationships among these variables involve the analyst in enormous complexity and uncertainty. There is little tested theory to inform the analyst concerning which of the myriad pieces of information are most important and how they should be combined to arrive at probabilistic judgments.

In the absence of any agreed-upon analytical schema, analysts are left to their own devices. They interpret information with the aid of mental models that are largely implicit rather than explicit. Assumptions concerning political forces and processes in the subject country may not be apparent even to the analyst. Such models are not representative of an analytical consensus. Other analysts examining the same data may well reach different conclusions, or reach the same conclusions but for different reasons. This analysis is conceptually driven, because the outcome depends at least as much upon the conceptual framework employed to analyze the data as it does upon the data itself.

To illustrate further the distinction between data-driven and conceptually driven analysis, it is useful to consider the function of the analyst responsible for current intelligence, especially current political intelligence as distinct from longer term research. The daily routine is driven by the incoming wire service news, embassy cables, and clandestine-source reporting from overseas that must be interpreted for dissemination to consumers throughout the Intelligence Community. Although current intelligence reporting is driven by incoming information, this is not what is meant by data-driven analysis. On the contrary, the current intelligence analyst's task is often extremely concept-driven. The analyst must provide immediate interpretation of the latest, often unexpected events. Apart from his or her store of background information, the analyst may have no data other than the initial, usually incomplete report. Under these circumstances, interpretation is based upon an implicit mental model of how and why events normally transpire in the country for which the analyst is responsible. Accuracy of judgment depends almost exclusively upon accuracy of the mental model, for there is little other basis for judgment.

It is necessary to consider how this mental model gets tested against reality, and how it can be changed to improve the accuracy of analytical judgment. Two things make it hard to change one's mental model. The first is the nature of human perception and information-processing. The second is the difficulty, in many fields, of learning what truly is an accurate model.

Partly because of the nature of human perception and information-processing, beliefs of all types tend to resist change. This is especially true of the implicit assumptions and supposedly self-evident truths that play an important role in forming mental models. Analysts are often surprised to learn that what are to them self-evident truths are by no means self-evident to others, or that self-evident truth at one point in time may be commonly regarded as uninformed assumption 10 years later.

Information that is consistent with an existing mind-set is perceived and processed easily and reinforces existing beliefs. Because the mind strives instinctively for consistency, information that is inconsistent with an existing mental image tends to be overlooked, perceived in a distorted manner, or rationalized to fit existing assumptions and beliefs.[62]

Learning to make better judgments through experience assumes systematic feedback on the accuracy of previous judgments and an ability to link the accuracy of a judgment with the particular configuration of variables that prompted an analyst to make that judgment. In practice, intelligence analysts get little systematic feedback, and even when they learn that an event they had foreseen has actually occurred or failed to occur, they typically do not know for certain whether this happened for the reasons they had foreseen. Thus, an analyst's personal experience may be a poor guide to revision of his or her mental mode.[63]

MOSAIC THEORY OF ANALYSIS

Understanding of the analytic process has been distorted by the mosaic metaphor commonly used to describe it. According to the mosaic theory of intelligence, small pieces of information are collected that, when put together like a mosaic or jigsaw puzzle, eventually enable analysts to perceive a clear picture of reality. The analogy suggests that accurate estimates depend primarily upon having all the pieces, that is, upon accurate and relatively complete information. It is important to collect and store the small pieces of information, as these are the raw material from which the picture is made; one never knows when it will be possible for an astute analyst to fit a piece into the puzzle. Part of the rationale for large technical intelligence collection systems is rooted in this mosaic theory.

Insights from cognitive psychology suggest that intelligence analysts do not work this way and that the most difficult analytical tasks cannot be approached in this manner. Analysts commonly find pieces that appear to fit many different pictures. Instead of a picture emerging from putting all the pieces together, analysts typically form a picture first and then select the pieces to fit. Accurate estimates depend at least as much upon the mental model used in forming the picture as upon the number of pieces of the puzzle that have been collected.

A more accurate analogy for describing how intelligence analysis should work is medical diagnosis. The doctor observes indicators (symptoms) of what is happening, uses his or her specialized knowledge of how the body works to develop hypotheses that might explain these observations, conducts tests to collect additional information to evaluate the hypotheses, then makes a diagnosis. This medical analogy focuses attention on the ability to identify and evaluate all plausible hypotheses. Collection is focused narrowly on information that will help to discriminate the relative probability of alternate hypothesis.

To the extent that this medical analogy is the more appropriate guide to understanding the analytical process, there are implications for the allocation of limited intelligence resources. While analysis and collection are both important, the medical analogy attributes more value to analysis and less to collection than the mosaic metaphor.

CONCLUSIONS

To the leaders and managers of intelligence who seek an improved intelligence product, these findings offer a reminder that this goal can be achieved by improving analysis as well as collection. There appear to be inherent practical limits on how much can be gained by efforts to improve collection. By contrast, an open and fertile field exists for imaginative efforts to improve analysis.

These efforts should focus on improving the mental models employed by analysts to interpret information and the analytical processes used to evaluate it. While this will be difficult to achieve, it is so critical to effective intelligence analysis that even small improvements could have large benefits. Specific recommendations are included the next three chapters and in Chapter 14, "Improving Intelligence Analysis."

Chapter 6

KEEPING AN OPEN MIND

SUMMARY

Minds are like parachutes. They only function when they are open. After reviewing how and why thinking gets channeled into mental ruts, this chapter looks at mental tools to help analysts keep an open mind, question assumptions, see different perspectives, develop new ideas, and recognize when it is time to change their minds.

A new idea is the beginning, not the end, of the creative process. It must jump over many hurdles before being embraced as an organizational product or solution. The organizational climate plays a crucial role in determining whether new ideas bubble to the surface or are suppressed.

Major intelligence failures are usually caused by failures of analysis, not failures of collection. Relevant information is discounted, misinterpreted, ignored, rejected, or overlooked because it fails to fit a prevailing mental model or mind-set.[64] The "signals" are lost in the "noise."[65] How can we ensure that analysts remain open to new experience and recognize when long-held views or conventional wisdom need to be revised in response to a changing world?

Beliefs, assumptions, concepts, and information retrieved from memory form a mind-set or mental model that guides perception and processing of new information. The nature of the intelligence business forces us to deal with issues at an early stage when hard information is incomplete. If there were no gaps in the information on an issue or situation, and no ambiguity, it would not be an interesting intelligence problem. When information is lacking, analysts often have no choice but to lean heavily on prior beliefs and assumptions about how and why events normally transpire in a given country.

A mind-set is neither good nor bad. It is unavoidable. It is, in essence, a distillation of all that analysts think they know about a subject. It forms a lens through which they perceive the world, and once formed, it resists change.

UNDERSTANDING MENTAL RUTS

Chapter 3 on memory suggested thinking of information in memory as somehow interconnected like a massive, multidimensional spider web. It is possible to connect any point within this web to any other point. When analysts connect the same points frequently, they form a path that makes it easier to take that route in the future. Once they start thinking along certain channels, they tend to continue thinking the same way and the path may become a rut. The path seems like the obvious and natural way to go. Information and concepts located near that path are readily available, so the same images keep coming up. Information not located near that path is less likely to come to mind.

Talking about breaking mind-sets, or creativity, or even just openness to new information is really talking about spinning new links and new paths through the web of memory. These are links among facts and concepts, or between schemata for organizing facts or concepts, that were not directly connected or only weakly connected before.

New ideas result from the association of old elements in new combinations. Previously remote elements of thought suddenly become associated in a new and useful combination.[66] When the linkage is made, the light dawns. This ability to bring previously unrelated information and ideas together in meaningful ways is what marks the open-minded, imaginative, creative analyst.

To illustrate how the mind works, consider my personal experience with a kind of mental block familiar to all analysts--writer's block. I often need to break a mental block when writing. Everything is going along fine until I come to one paragraph and get stuck. I write something down, know it is not quite right, but just cannot think of a better way to say it. However I try to change the paragraph, it still comes out basically the same way. My thinking has become channeled, and I cannot break out of that particular thought pattern to write it differently.

A common response to this problem is to take a break, work on something different for a while, and come back to the difficult portion later. With the passage of time, the path becomes less pronounced and it becomes easier to make other connections.

I have found another solution. I force myself to talk about it out loud. I close the door to my office--I am embarrassed to have anyone hear me talking to myself--and then stand up and walk around and talk. I say, okay, "What is the point of this paragraph? What are you trying to communicate?" I answer myself out loud as though talking to someone else. "The point I am trying to get across is that ...," and then it just comes. Saying it out loud breaks the block, and words start coming together in different ways.

Recent research explains why this happens. Scientists have learned that written language and spoken language are processed in different parts of the brain.[67] They activate different neurons.

Problem-Solving Exercise

Before discussing how analysts can keep their minds open to new information, let us warm up to this topic with a brief exercise. Without lifting pencil from paper, draw no more than four straight lines that will cross through all nine dots in Figure 6. [68]

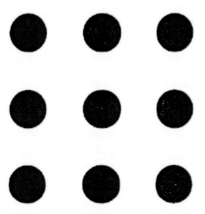

Figure 6

After trying to solve the puzzle on your own, refer to the end of this chapter for answers and further discussion. Then consider that intelligence analysis is too often limited by similar, unconscious, self-imposed constraints or "cages of the mind."

You do not need to be constrained by conventional wisdom. It is often wrong. You do not *necessarily* need to be constrained by existing policies. They can sometimes be changed if you show a good reason for doing so. You do not *necessarily* need to be constrained by the specific analytical requirement you were given. The policymaker who originated the requirement may not have thought through his or her needs or the requirement may be somewhat garbled as it passes down through several echelons to you to do the work. You may have a better understanding than the policymaker of what he or she needs, or should have, or what is possible to do. You should not hesitate to go back up the chain of command with a suggestion for doing something a little different than what was asked for.

MENTAL TOOLS

People use various physical tools such as a hammer and saw to enhance their capacity to perform various physical tasks. People can also use simple mental tools to enhance their ability to perform mental tasks. These tools help overcome limitations in human mental machinery for perception, memory, and inference. The next few sections of this chapter discuss mental tools for opening analysts' minds to new ideas, while the next one (Chapter 7) deals with mental tools for structuring complex analytical problems.

Questioning Assumptions

It is a truism that analysts need to question their assumptions. Experience tells us that when analytical judgments turn out to be wrong, it usually was not because the information was wrong. It was because an analyst made one or more faulty assumptions that went unchallenged. The problem is that analysts cannot question everything, so where do they focus their attention?

Sensitivity Analysis
One approach is to do an informal sensitivity analysis. How sensitive is the ultimate judgment to changes in any of the major variables or driving forces in the analysis? Those linchpin assumptions that drive the analysis are

the ones that need to be questioned. Analysts should ask themselves what could happen to make any of these assumptions out of date, and how they can know this has not already happened. They should try to disprove their assumptions rather than confirm them. If an analyst cannot think of anything that would cause a change of mind, his or her mind-set may be so deeply entrenched that the analyst cannot see the conflicting evidence. One advantage of the competing hypotheses approach discussed in Chapter 8 is that it helps identify the linchpin assumptions that swing a conclusion in one direction or another.

Identify Alternative Models

Analysts should try to identify alternative models, conceptual frameworks, or interpretations of the data by seeking out individuals who disagree with them rather than those who agree. Most people do not do that very often. It is much more comfortable to talk with people in one's own office who share the same basic mind-set. There are a few things that can be done as a matter of policy, and that have been done in some offices in the past, to help overcome this tendency.

At least one Directorate of Intelligence component, for example, has had a peer review process in which none of the reviewers was from the branch that produced the report. The rationale for this was that an analyst's immediate colleagues and supervisor(s) are likely to share a common mind-set. Hence these are the individuals least likely to raise fundamental issues challenging the validity of the analysis. To avoid this mind-set problem, each research report was reviewed by a committee of three analysts from other branches handling other countries or issues. None of them had specialized knowledge of the subject. They were, however, highly accomplished analysts. Precisely because they had not been immersed in the issue in question, they were better able to identify hidden assumptions and other alternatives, and to judge whether the analysis adequately supported the conclusions.

Be Wary of Mirror Images

One kind of assumption an analyst should always recognize and question is mirror-imaging--filling gaps in the analyst's own knowledge by assuming that the other side is likely to act in a certain way because that is how the US would act under similar circumstances. To say, "if I were a Russian intelligence officer ..." or "if I were running the Indian Government ..." is mirror-imaging. Analysts may have to do that when they do not know how the Russian intelligence officer or the Indian Government is really thinking. But mirror-imaging leads to dangerous assumptions, because people in other cultures *do not* think the way we do. The frequent assumption that they do is what Adm. David Jeremiah, after reviewing the Intelligence Community failure to predict India's nuclear weapons testing, termed the "everybody-thinks-like-us mind-set."[69]

Failure to understand that others perceive their national interests differently from the way we perceive those interests is a constant source of problems in intelligence analysis. In 1977, for example, the Intelligence Community was faced with evidence of what appeared to be a South African nuclear weapons test site. Many in the Intelligence Community, especially those least knowledgeable about South Africa, tended to dismiss this evidence on the grounds that "Pretoria would not want a nuclear weapon, because there is no enemy they could effectively use it on."[70] The US perspective on what is in another country's national interest is usually irrelevant in intelligence analysis. Judgment must be based on how the other country perceives its national interest. If the analyst cannot gain insight into what the other country is thinking, mirror-imaging may be the only alternative, but analysts should never get caught putting much confidence in that kind of judgment.

Seeing Different Perspectives

Another problem area is looking at familiar data from a different perspective. If you play chess, you know you can see your own options pretty well. It is much more difficult to see all the pieces on the board as your opponent sees them, and to anticipate how your opponent will react to your move. That is the situation analysts are in when they try to see how the US Government's actions look from another country's perspective. Analysts constantly have to move back and forth, first seeing the situation from the US perspective and then from the other country's perspective. This is difficult to do, as you experienced with the picture of the old woman/young woman in Chapter 2 on perception.

Several techniques for seeing alternative perspectives exploit the general principle of coming at the problem from a different direction and asking different questions. These techniques break your existing mind-set by causing you to play a different and unaccustomed role.

Thinking Backwards

One technique for exploring new ground is thinking backwards. As an intellectual exercise, start with an assumption that some event you did not expect has actually occurred. Then, put yourself into the future, looking back to explain how this could have happened. Think what must have happened six months or a year earlier to set the stage for that outcome, what must have happened six months or a year before that to prepare the way, and so on back to the present.

Thinking backwards changes the focus from whether something might happen to how it might happen. Putting yourself into the future creates a different perspective that keeps you from getting anchored in the present. Analysts will often find, to their surprise, that they can construct a quite plausible scenario for an event they had previously thought unlikely. Thinking backwards is particularly helpful for events that have a low probability but very serious consequences should they occur, such as a collapse or overthrow of the Saudi monarchy.

Crystal Ball

The crystal ball approach works in much the same way as thinking backwards.[71] Imagine that a "perfect" intelligence source (such as a crystal ball) has told you a certain assumption is wrong. You must then develop a scenario to explain how this could be true. If you can develop a plausible scenario, this suggests your assumption is open to some question.

Role playing

Role playing is commonly used to overcome constraints and inhibitions that limit the range of one's thinking. Playing a role changes "where you sit." It also gives one license to think and act differently. Simply trying to imagine how another leader or country will think and react, which analysts do frequently, is not role playing. One must actually act out the role and become, in a sense, the person whose role is assumed. It is only "living" the role that breaks an analyst's normal mental set and permits him or her to relate facts and ideas to each other in ways that differ from habitual patterns. An analyst cannot be expected to do this alone; some group interaction is required, with different analysts playing different roles, usually in the context of an organized simulation or game.

Most of the gaming done in the Defense Department and in the academic world is rather elaborate and requires substantial preparatory work. It does not have to be that way. The preparatory work can be avoided by starting the game with the current situation already known to analysts, rather than with a notional scenario that participants have to learn. Just one notional intelligence report is sufficient to start the action in the game. In my experience, it is possible to have a useful political game in just one day with almost no investment in preparatory work.

Gaming gives no "right" answer, but it usually causes the players to see some things in a new light. Players become very conscious that "where you stand depends on where you sit." By changing roles, the participants see the problem in a different context. This frees the mind to think differently.

Devil's Advocate

A devil's advocate is someone who defends a minority point of view. He or she may not necessarily agree with that view, but may choose or be assigned to represent it as strenuously as possible. The goal is to expose conflicting interpretations and show how alternative assumptions and images make the world look different. It often requires time, energy, and commitment to see how the world looks from a different perspective. [72]

Imagine that you are the boss at a US facility overseas and are worried about the possibility of a terrorist attack. A standard staff response would be to review existing measures and judge their adequacy. There might well be pressure--subtle or otherwise--from those responsible for such arrangements to find them satisfactory. An alternative or supplementary approach would be to name an individual or small group as a devil's advocate assigned to develop actual plans for launching such an attack. The assignment to think like a terrorist liberates the designated person(s) to think unconventionally and be less inhibited about finding weaknesses in the system that might embarrass colleagues, because uncovering any such weaknesses is the assigned task.

Devil's advocacy has a controversial history in the Intelligence Community. Suffice it to say that some competition between conflicting views is healthy and must be encouraged; all-out political battle is counterproductive.

Recognizing when to Change Your Mind

As a general rule, people are too slow to change an established view, as opposed to being too willing to change. The human mind is conservative. It resists change. Assumptions that worked well in the past continue to be applied to new situations long after they have become outmoded.

Learning from Surprise

A study of senior managers in industry identified how some successful managers counteract this conservative bent. They do it, according to the study,

By paying attention to their feelings of surprise when a particular fact does not fit their prior understanding, and then by highlighting rather than denying the novelty. Although surprise made them feel uncomfortable, it made them take the cause [of the surprise] seriously and inquire into it....Rather than deny, downplay, or ignore disconfirmation [of their prior view], successful senior managers often treat it as friendly and in a way cherish the discomfort surprise creates. As a result, these managers often perceive novel situations early on and in a frame of mind relatively undistorted by hidebound notions.[73]

Analysts should keep a record of unexpected events and think hard about what they might mean, not disregard them or explain them away. It is important to consider whether these surprises, however small, are consistent with some alternative hypothesis. One unexpected event may be easy to disregard, but a pattern of surprises may be the first clue that your understanding of what is happening requires some adjustment, is at best incomplete, and may be quite wrong.

Strategic Assumptions vs. Tactical Indicators

Abraham Ben-Zvi analyzed five cases of intelligence failure to foresee a surprise attack.[74] He made a useful distinction between estimates based on strategic assumptions and estimates based on tactical indications. Examples of strategic assumptions include the US belief in 1941 that Japan wished to avoid war at all costs because it recognized US military superiority, and the Israeli belief in 1973 that the Arabs would not attack Israel until they obtained sufficient air power to secure control of the skies. A more recent instance was the 1998 Indian nuclear test, which was widely viewed as a surprise and, at least in part, as a failure by the experts to warn of an impending test. The incorrect strategic assumption was that the new Indian Government would be dissuaded from testing nuclear weapons for fear of US economic sanctions.[75]

Tactical indicators are specific reports of preparations or intent to initiate hostile action or, in the recent Indian case, reports of preparations for a nuclear test. Ben-Zvi found that whenever strategic assumptions and tactical indicators of impending attack converged, an immediate threat was perceived and appropriate precautionary measures were taken. When discrepancies existed between tactical indicators and strategic assumptions in the five cases Ben-Zvi analyzed, the strategic assumptions always prevailed, and they were never reevaluated in the light of the increasing flow of contradictory information. Ben-Zvi concludes that tactical indicators should be given increased weight in the decisionmaking process. At a minimum, the emergence of tactical indicators that contradict our strategic assumption should trigger a higher level of intelligence alert. It may indicate that a bigger surprise is on the way.

Chapter 8, "Analysis of Competing Hypotheses," provides a framework for identifying surprises and weighing tactical indicators and other forms of current evidence against longstanding assumptions and beliefs.

Stimulating Creative Thinking

Imagination and creativity play important roles in intelligence analysis as in most other human endeavors. Intelligence judgments require the ability to imagine possible causes and outcomes of a current situation. All possible outcomes are not given. The analyst must think of them by imagining scenarios that explicate how they might come about. Similarly, imagination as well as knowledge is required to reconstruct how a problem appears from the viewpoint of a foreign government. Creativity is required to question things that have long been taken for granted. The fact that apples fall from trees was well known to everyone. Newton's creative genius was to ask "why?" Intelligence analysts, too, are expected to raise new questions that lead to the identification of previously unrecognized relationships or to possible outcomes that had not previously been foreseen.

A creative analytical product shows a flair for devising imaginative or innovative--but also accurate and effective--ways to fulfill any of the major requirements of analysis: gathering information, analyzing information, documenting evidence, and/or presenting conclusions. Tapping unusual sources of data, asking new questions, applying unusual analytic methods, and developing new types of products or new ways of fitting analysis to the needs of consumers are all examples of creative activity.

A person's intelligence, as measured by IQ tests, has little to do with creativity, but the organizational environment exercises a major influence. New but appropriate ideas are most likely to arise in an organizational climate that nurtures their development and communication.

The old view that creativity is something one is born with, and that it cannot be taught or developed, is largely untrue. While native talent, per se, is important and may be immutable, it is possible to learn to employ one's innate talents more productively. With understanding, practice, and conscious effort, analysts can learn to produce more imaginative, innovative, creative work.

There is a large body of literature on creativity and how to stimulate it. At least a half-dozen different methods have been developed for teaching, facilitating, or liberating creative thinking. All the methods for teaching or facilitating creativity are based on the assumption that the *process* of thinking can be separated from the *content* of thought. One learns mental strategies that can be applied to any subject.

It is not our purpose here to review commercially available programs for enhancing creativity. Such programmatic approaches can be applied more meaningfully to problems of new product development, advertising, or management than to intelligence analysis. It is relevant, however, to discuss several key principles and techniques that these programs have in common, and that individual intelligence analysts or groups of analysts can apply in their work.

Intelligence analysts must generate ideas concerning potential causes or explanations of events, policies that might be pursued or actions taken by a foreign government, possible outcomes of an existing situation, and variables that will influence which outcome actually comes to pass. Analysts also need help to jog them out of mental ruts, to stimulate their memories and imaginations, and to perceive familiar events from a new perspective.

Here are some of the principles and techniques of creative thinking that can be applied to intelligence analysis.

Deferred Judgment

The principle of deferred judgment is undoubtedly the most important. The idea-generation phase of analysis should be separated from the idea-evaluation phase, with evaluation deferred until all possible ideas have been brought out. This approach runs contrary to the normal procedure of thinking of ideas and evaluating them concurrently. Stimulating the imagination and critical thinking are both important, but they do not mix well. A judgmental attitude dampens the imagination, whether it manifests itself as self-censorship of one's own ideas or fear of critical evaluation by colleagues or supervisors. Idea generation should be a freewheeling, unconstrained, uncritical process.

New ideas are, by definition, unconventional, and therefore likely to be suppressed, either consciously or unconsciously, unless they are born in a secure and protected environment. Critical judgment should be suspended until after the idea-generation stage of analysis has been completed. A series of ideas should be written down and then evaluated later. This applies to idea searching by individuals as well as brainstorming in a group. Get all the ideas out on the table before evaluating any of them.

Quantity Leads to Quality

A second principle is that quantity of ideas eventually leads to quality. This is based on the assumption that the first ideas that come to mind will be those that are most common or usual. It is necessary to run through these conventional ideas before arriving at original or different ones. People have habitual ways of thinking, ways that they continue to use because they have seemed successful in the past. It may well be that these habitual responses, the ones that come first to mind, are the best responses and that further search is unnecessary. In looking for usable new ideas, however, one should seek to generate as many ideas as possible before evaluating any of them.

No Self-Imposed Constraints

A third principle is that thinking should be allowed--indeed encouraged--to range as freely as possible. It is necessary to free oneself from self-imposed constraints, whether they stem from analytical habit, limited perspective, social norms, emotional blocks, or whatever.

Cross-Fertilization of Ideas

A fourth principle of creative problem-solving is that cross-fertilization of ideas is important and necessary. Ideas should be combined with each other to form more and even better ideas. If creative thinking involves forging new links between previously unrelated or weakly related concepts, then creativity will be stimulated by any activity that brings more concepts into juxtaposition with each other in fresh ways. Interaction with other analysts is one basic mechanism for this. As a general rule, people generate more creative ideas when teamed up with others; they help to build and develop each other's ideas. Personal interaction stimulates new associations between ideas. It also induces greater effort and helps maintain concentration on the task.

These favorable comments on group processes are not meant to encompass standard committee meetings or coordination processes that force consensus based on the lowest common denominator of agreement. My positive words about group interaction apply primarily to brainstorming sessions aimed at generating new ideas and in which, according to the first principle discussed above, all criticism and evaluation are deferred until after the idea generation stage is completed.

Thinking things out alone also has its advantages: individual thought tends to be more structured and systematic than interaction within a group. Optimal results come from alternating between individual thinking and team effort, using group interaction to generate ideas that supplement individual thought. A diverse group is clearly preferable to a homogeneous one. Some group participants should be analysts who are not close to the problem, inasmuch as their ideas are more likely to reflect different insights.

Idea Evaluation

All creativity techniques are concerned with stimulating the flow of ideas. There are no comparable techniques for determining which ideas are best. The procedures are, therefore, aimed at idea generation rather than idea evaluation. The same procedures do aid in evaluation, however, in the sense that ability to generate more alternatives helps one see more potential consequences, repercussions, and effects that any single idea or action might entail.

ORGANIZATIONAL ENVIRONMENT

A new idea is not the end product of the creative process. Rather, it is the beginning of what is sometimes a long and tortuous process of translating an idea into an innovative product. The idea must be developed, evaluated, and communicated to others, and this process is influenced by the organizational setting in which it transpires. The potentially useful new idea must pass over a number of hurdles before it is embraced as an organizational product.

The following paragraphs describe in some detail research conducted by Frank Andrews to investigate the relationship among creative ability, organizational setting, and innovative research products.[76] The subjects of this research were 115 scientists, each of whom had directed a research project dealing with social-psychological aspects of disease. These scientists were given standardized tests that measure creative ability and intelligence. They were also asked to fill out an extensive questionnaire concerning the environment in which their research was conducted. A panel of judges composed of the leading scientists in the field of medical sociology was asked to evaluate the principal published results from each of the 115 research projects.

Judges evaluated the research results on the basis of productivity and innovation. Productivity was defined as the "extent to which the research represents an addition to knowledge along established lines of research or as extensions of previous theory." Innovativeness was defined as "additions to knowledge through new lines of research or the development of new theoretical statements of findings that were not explicit in previous theory.[77] Innovation, in other words, involved raising new questions and developing new approaches to the acquisition of knowledge, as distinct from working productively within an already established framework. This same definition applies to innovation in intelligence analysis.

Andrews found virtually no relationship between the scientists' creative ability and the innovativeness of their research. (There was also no relationship between level of intelligence and innovativeness.) Those who scored high on tests of creative ability did not necessarily receive high ratings from the judges evaluating the innovativeness of their work. A possible explanation is that either creative ability or innovation, or both, were not measured accurately, but Andrews argues persuasively for another view. Various social and psychological factors have so great an effect on the steps needed to translate creative ability into an innovative research product that there is no measurable effect traceable to creative ability alone. In order to document this conclusion, Andrews analyzed data from the questionnaires in which the scientists described their work environment.

Andrews found that scientists possessing more creative ability produced more innovative work only under the following favorable conditions:

- When the scientist perceived himself or herself as responsible for initiating new activities. The opportunity for innovation, and the encouragement of it, are--not surprisingly--important variables.
- When the scientist had considerable control over decisionmaking concerning his or her research program--in other words, the freedom to set goals, hire research assistants, and expend funds. Under these circumstances, a new idea is less likely to be snuffed out before it can be developed into a creative and useful product.
- When the scientist felt secure and comfortable in his or her professional role. New ideas are often disruptive, and pursuing them carries the risk of failure. People are more likely to advance new ideas if they feel secure in their positions.
- When the scientist's administrative superior "stayed out of the way." Research is likely to be more innovative when the superior limits himself or herself to support and facilitation rather than direct involvement.

- When the project was relatively small with respect to the number of people involved, budget, and duration. Small size promotes flexibility, and this in turn is more conducive to creativity.
- When the scientist engaged in other activities, such as teaching or administration, in addition to the research project. Other work may provide useful stimulation or help one identify opportunities for developing or implementing new ideas. Some time away from the task, or an incubation period, is generally recognized as part of the creative process."

The importance of any one of these factors was not very great, but their impact was cumulative. The presence of all or most of these conditions exerted a strongly favorable influence on the creative process. Conversely, the absence of these conditions made it quite unlikely that even highly creative scientists could develop their new ideas into innovative research results. Under unfavorable conditions, the most creatively inclined scientists produced even less innovative work than their less imaginative colleagues, presumably because they experienced greater frustration with their work environment.

In summary, some degree of innate creative talent may be a necessary precondition for innovative work, but it is unlikely to be of much value unless the organizational environment in which that work is done nurtures the development and communication of new ideas. Under unfavorable circumstances, an individual's creative impulses probably will find expression outside the organization.

There are, of course, exceptions to the rule. Some creativity occurs even in the face of intense opposition. A hostile environment can be stimulating, enlivening, and challenging. Some people gain satisfaction from viewing themselves as lonely fighters in the wilderness, but when it comes to conflict between a large organization and a creative individual within it, the organization generally wins.

Recognizing the role of organizational environment in stimulating or suppressing creativity points the way to one obvious set of measures to enhance creative organizational performance. Managers of analysis, from first-echelon supervisors to the Director of Central Intelligence, should take steps to strengthen and broaden the perception among analysts that new ideas are welcome. This is not easy; creativity implies criticism of that which already exists. It is, therefore, inherently disruptive of established ideas and organizational practices.

Particularly within his or her own office, an analyst needs to enjoy a sense of security, so that partially developed ideas may be expressed and bounced off others as sounding boards with minimal fear of criticism or ridicule for deviating from established orthodoxy. At its inception, a new idea is frail and vulnerable. It needs to be nurtured, developed, and tested in a protected environment before being exposed to the harsh reality of public criticism. It is the responsibility of an analyst's immediate supervisor and office colleagues to provide this sheltered environment.

CONCLUSIONS

Creativity, in the sense of new and useful ideas, is at least as important in intelligence analysis as in any other human endeavor. Procedures to enhance innovative thinking are not new. Creative thinkers have employed them successfully for centuries. The only new elements--and even they may not be new anymore--are the grounding of these procedures in psychological theory to explain how and why they work, and their formalization in systematic creativity programs.

Learning creative problem-solving techniques does not change an analyst's native-born talents but helps an analyst achieve his or her full potential. Most people have the ability to be more innovative than they themselves realize. The effectiveness of these procedures depends, in large measure, upon the analyst's motivation, drive, and perseverance in taking the time required for thoughtful analysis despite the pressures of day-to-day duties, mail, and current intelligence reporting.

A questioning attitude is a prerequisite to a successful search for new ideas. Any analyst who is confident that he or she already knows the answer, and that this answer has not changed recently, is unlikely to produce innovative or imaginative work. Another prerequisite to creativity is sufficient strength of character to suggest new ideas to others, possibly at the expense of being rejected or even ridiculed on occasion. "The ideas of creative people often lead them into direct conflict with the trends of their time, and they need the courage to be able to stand alone."[78]

SOLUTIONS TO PUZZLE PRESENTED IN FIGURE 6

The nine-dots puzzle illustrated in Figure 6 above and earlier in this chapter is difficult to solve only if one defines the problem to narrowly. A surprising number of people assume they are not supposed to let the pencil go outside an imaginary square drawn around the nine dots.

Figure 6

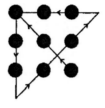

Figure 7

This unconscious constraint exists only in the mind of the problem-solver; it is not specified in the definition of the problem. With no limit on the length of lines, it should be relatively easy to come up with the answer shown in Figure 7.

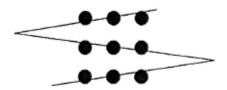

Figure 8

Another common, unconscious constraint is the assumption that the lines must pass through the center of the dots. This constraint, too, exists only in the mind of the problem solver. Without it, the three-line solution in Figure 8 becomes rather obvious.

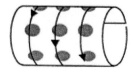

Figure 9

A more subtle and certainly more pervasive mental block is the assumption that such problems must be solved within a two-dimensional-plane. By rolling the paper to form a cylinder, it becomes possible to draw a single straight line that spirals through all nine dots, as in Figure 9.

Chapter 7

STRUCTURING ANALYTICAL PROBLEMS

SUMMARY

This chapter discusses various structures for decomposing and externalizing complex analytical problems when we cannot keep all the relevant factors in the forefront of our consciousness at the same time.

Decomposition means breaking a problem down into its component parts. Externalization means getting the problem out of our heads and into some visible form that we can work with.

The discussion of working memory in Chapter 3 indicated that "The Magic Number Seven--Plus or Minus Two"[79] is the number of things most people can keep in working memory at one time. To experience firsthand this limitation on working memory while doing a mental task, try multiplying in your head any pair of two-digit numbers- for example, 46 times 78. On paper, this is a simple problem, but most people cannot keep track of that many numbers in their head.

The limited capacity of working memory is the source of many problems in doing intelligence analysis. It is useful to consider just how complicated analysis can get, and how complexity might outstrip your working memory and impede your ability to make accurate judgments. Figure 10 illustrates how complexity increases geometrically as the number of variables in an analytical problem increases. The four-sided square shows that when a problem has just four variables, there are six possible interrelationships between those variables. With the pentagon, the five variables have 10 possible interrelationships. With six and eight variables, respectively, there are 15 and 28 possible interrelationships between variables.

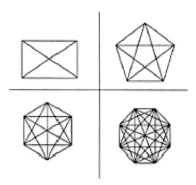

Figure 10. The number of possible relationships between variables grows geometrically as the number of variables increases.

There are two basic tools for dealing with complexity in analysis--decomposition and externalization.

Decomposition means breaking a problem down into its component parts. That is, indeed, the essence of analysis. Webster's Dictionary defines analysis as division of a complex whole into its parts or elements.[80]

The spirit of decision analysis is to divide and conquer: Decompose a complex problem into simpler problems, get one's thinking straight in these simpler problems, paste these analyses together with a logical glue ...[81]

Externalization means getting the decomposed problem out of one's head and down on paper or on a computer screen in some simplified form that shows the main variables, parameters, or elements of the problem and how they relate to each other. Writing down the multiplication problem, 46 times 78, is a very simple example of externalizing an analytical problem. When it is down on paper, one can easily manipulate one part of the problem at a time and often be more accurate than when trying to multiply the numbers in one's head.

I call this drawing a picture of your problem. Others call it making a model of your problem. It can be as simple as just making lists pro and con.

This recommendation to compensate for limitations of working memory by decomposing and externalizing analytical problems is not new. The following quote is from a letter Benjamin Franklin wrote in 1772 to the great British scientist Joseph Priestley, the discoverer of oxygen:

In the affair of so much importance to you, wherein you ask my advice, I cannot for want of sufficient premises, advise you what to determine, but if you please I will tell you how. When those difficult cases occur, they are difficult, chiefly because while we have them under consideration, all the reasons pro and con are not present to the mind at the same time, but sometimes one set present themselves, and at other times another, the first being out of sight. Hence the various purposes or inclinations that alternatively prevail, and the uncertainty that perplexes us.

To get over this, my way is to divide half a sheet of paper by a line into two columns; writing over the one Pro, and over the other Con. Then, during three or four days of consideration, I put down under the different heads short hints of the different motives, that at different times occur to me, for or against the measure.

When I have thus got them all together in one view, I endeavor to estimate their respective weights; and where I find two, one on each side, that seem equal, I strike them both out. If I find a reason pro equal to some two reasons con, I strike out the three . . . and thus proceeding I find at length where the balance lies; and if, after a day or two of further consideration, nothing new that is of importance occurs on either side, I come to a determination accordingly.

And, though the weight of reasons cannot be taken with the precision of algebraic quantities, yet when each is thus considered, separately and comparatively, and the whole lies before me, I think I can judge better, and am less liable to make a rash step, and in fact I have found great advantage from this kind of equation. . . . [82]

It is noteworthy that Franklin over 200 years ago ident2ified the problem of limited working memory and how it affects one's ability to make judgments. As Franklin noted, decision problems are difficult because people cannot keep all the pros and cons in mind at the same time. We focus first on one set of arguments and then on another, "...hence the various purposes and inclinations that alternatively prevail, and the uncertainty that perplexes us."

Franklin also identified the solution--getting all the pros and cons out of his head and onto paper in some visible, shorthand form. The fact that this topic was part of the dialogue between such illustrious individuals reflects the type of people who use such analytical tools. These are not aids to be used by weak analysts but unneeded by the strong. Basic limitations of working memory affect everyone. It is the more astute and careful analysts who are most conscious of this and most likely to recognize the value gained by applying these very simple tools.

Putting ideas into visible form ensures that they will last. They will lie around for days goading you into having further thoughts. Lists are effective because they exploit people's tendency to be a bit compulsive--we want to keep adding to them. They let us get the obvious and habitual answers out of the way, so that we can add to the list by thinking of other ideas beyond those that came first to mind. One specialist in creativity has observed that "for the purpose of moving our minds, pencils can serve as crowbars"[83]-- just by writing things down and making lists that stimulate new associations.

With the key elements of a problem written down in some abbreviated form, it is far easier to work with each of the parts while still keeping the problem as a whole in view. Analysts can generally take account of more factors than when making a global judgment. They can manipulate individual elements of the problem to examine the many alternatives available through rearranging, combining, or modifying them. Variables may be given more weight or deleted, causal relationships reconceptualized, or conceptual categories redefined. Such thoughts may arise spontaneously, but they are more likely to occur when an analyst looks at each element, one by one, and asks questions designed to encourage and facilitate consideration of alternative interpretations.

PROBLEM STRUCTURE

Anything that has parts also has a structure that relates these parts to each other. One of the first steps in doing analysis is to determine an appropriate structure for the analytical problem, so that one can then identify the various parts and begin assembling information on them. Because there are many different kinds of analytical problems, there are also many different ways to structure analysis.

Lists such as Franklin made are one of the simplest structures. An intelligence analyst might make lists of relevant variables, early warning indicators, alternative explanations, possible outcomes, factors a foreign leader will need to take into account when making a decision, or arguments for and against a given explanation or outcome.

Other tools for structuring a problem include outlines, tables, diagrams, trees, and matrices, with many sub-species of each. For example, trees include decision trees and fault trees. Diagrams includes causal diagrams, influence diagrams, flow charts, and cognitive maps.

Consideration of all those tools is beyond the scope of this book, but several such tools are discussed. Chapter 11, "Biases in Perception of Cause and Effect," has a section on Illusory Correlation that uses a (2x2) contingency table to structure analysis of the question: Is deception most likely when the stakes are very high? Chapter 8, "Analysis of Competing Hypotheses," is arguably the most useful chapter in this book. It recommends using a matrix to array evidence for and against competing hypotheses to explain what is happening now or estimate what may happen in the future.

The discussion below also uses a matrix to illustrate decomposition and externalization and is intended to prepare you for the next chapter on "Analysis of Competing Hypotheses." It demonstrates how to apply these tools to a type of decision commonly encountered in our personal lives.

Car Purchase Matrix

In choosing among alternative purchases, such as when buying a car, a new computer, or a house, people often want to maximize their satisfaction on a number of sometimes-conflicting dimensions. They want a car at the lowest possible price, with the lowest maintenance cost, highest resale value, slickest styling, best handling, best gas mileage, largest trunk space, and so forth. They can't have it all, so they must decide what is most important and make tradeoffs. As Ben Franklin said, the choice is sometimes difficult. We vacillate between one choice and another, because we cannot keep in working memory at the same time all the characteristics of all the choices. We think first of one and then the other.

To handle this problem analytically, follow the divide-and-conquer principle and "draw a picture" of the problem as a whole that helps you identify and make the tradeoffs. The component parts of the car purchase problem are the cars you are considering buying and the attributes or dimensions you want to maximize. After identifying the desirable attributes that will influence your decision, weigh how each car stacks up on each attribute. A matrix is the appropriate tool for keeping track of your judgments about each car and each attribute, and then putting all the parts back together to make a decision.

Start by listing the important attributes you want to maximize, as shown for example in Figure 11.

Next, quantify the relative importance of each attribute by dividing 100 percent among them. In other words, ask yourself what percentage of the decision should be based on price, on styling, etc. This forces you to ask relevant questions and make decisions you might have glossed over if you had not broken the problem down in this manner. How important is price versus styling, really? Do you really care what it looks like from the outside, or are you mainly looking for comfort on the inside and how it drives? Should safety be included in your list of important attributes? Because poor gas mileage can be offset by lower maintenance cost for repairs, perhaps both should be combined into a single attribute called operating cost.

Price

Maintenance Cost

Styling

Gas Mileage

Comfort

Handling

Figure 11

Price	30%
Operating Cost	10%
Styling	20%
Comfort	20%
Handling	15%
Safety	5%
Total	100%

Figure 12

This step might produce a result similar to Figure 12, depending on your personal preferences. If you do this together with your spouse, the exact basis of any difference of opinion will become immediately apparent and can be quantified.

Next, identify the cars you are considering and judge how each one ranks on each of the six attributes shown in Figure 12. Set up a matrix as shown in Figure 13 and work across the rows of the matrix. For each attribute, take 10 points and divide it among the three cars based on how well they meet the requirements of that attribute. (This is the same as taking

100 percent and dividing it among the cars, but it keeps the numbers lower when you get to the next step.)

You now have a picture of your analytical problem--the comparative value you attribute to each of the principal attributes of a new car and a comparison of how various cars satisfy those desired attributes. If you have narrowed it down to three alternatives, your matrix will look something like Figure 13:

	%Value	Car 1	Car 2	Car 3
Price	30%	3.5%	3.0%	3.5%
Operating Cost	10%	3.5%	2.0%	4.5%
Styling	20%	2.5%	4.5%	3.0%
Comfort	20%	4.0%	2.5%	3.5%
Handling	15%	3.0%	4.0%	3.0%
Safety	5%	3.5%	2.5%	4%

Figure 13

When all the cells of the matrix have been filled in, you can then calculate which car best suits your preferences. Multiply the percentage value you assigned to each attribute by the value you assigned to that attribute for each car, which produces the result in Figure 14. If the percentage values you assigned to each attribute accurately reflect your preferences, and if each car has been analyzed accurately, the analysis shows you will gain more satisfaction from the purchase of Car 3 than either of the alternatives.

	%Value	Car 1	Car 2	Car 3
Price	30%	105	90	105
Operating Cost	10%	35	20	45
Styling	20%	50	90	60
Comfort	20%	80	50	70
Handling	15%	45	60	45
Safety	5%	17.5	12.5	20
Totals		332.5	322.5	345

Figure 14

At this point, you do a sensitivity analysis to determine whether plausible changes in some values in the matrix would swing the decision to a different car. Assume, for example, that your spouse places different values than you on the relative importance of price versus styling. You can insert your spouse's percentage values for those two attributes and see if that makes a difference in the decision. (For example, one could reduce the importance of price to 20 percent and increase styling to 30 percent. That is still not quite enough to switch the choice to Car 2, which rates highest on styling.)

There is a technical name for this type of analysis. It is called Multiattribute Utility Analysis, and there are complex computer programs for doing it. In simplified form, however, it requires only pencil and paper and high school arithmetic. It is an appropriate structure for any purchase decision in which you must make tradeoffs between multiple competing preferences.

CONCLUSIONS

The car purchase example was a warmup for the following chapter. It illustrates the difference between just sitting down and thinking about a problem and really *analyzing* a problem. The essence of analysis is breaking down a problem into its component parts, assessing each part separately, then putting the parts back together to make a decision. The matrix in this example forms a "picture" of a complex problem by getting it out of our head and onto paper in a logical form that enables you to consider each of the parts individually.

You certainly would not want to do this type of analysis for all your everyday personal decisions or for every intelligence judgment. You may wish to do it, however, for an especially important, difficult, or controversial judgment, or when you need to leave an audit trail showing how you arrived at a judgment. The next chapter applies decomposition, externalization, and the matrix structure to a common type of intelligence problem.

Chapter 8

ANALYSIS OF COMPETING HYPOTHESES

SUMMARY

Analysis of competing hypotheses, sometimes abbreviated ACH, is a tool to aid judgment on important issues requiring careful weighing of alternative explanations or conclusions. It helps an analyst overcome, or at least minimize, some of the cognitive limitations that make prescient intelligence analysis so difficult to achieve.

ACH is an eight-step procedure grounded in basic insights from cognitive psychology, decision analysis, and the scientific method. It is a surprisingly effective, proven process that helps analysts avoid common analytic pitfalls. Because of its thoroughness, it is particularly appropriate for controversial issues when analysts want to leave an audit trail to show what they considered and how they arrived at their judgment.[84]

When working on difficult intelligence issues, analysts are, in effect, choosing among several alternative hypotheses. Which of several possible explanations is the correct one? Which of several possible outcomes is the most likely one? As previously noted, this book uses the term "hypothesis" in its broadest sense as a potential explanation or conclusion that is to be tested by collecting and presenting evidence.

Analysis of competing hypotheses (ACH) requires an analyst to explicitly identify all the reasonable alternatives and have them compete against each other for the analyst's favor, rather than evaluating their plausibility one at a time.

The way most analysts go about their business is to pick out what they suspect intuitively is the most likely answer, then look at the available information from the point of view of whether or not it supports this answer.

If the evidence seems to support the favorite hypothesis, analysts pat themselves on the back ("See, I knew it all along!") and look no further. If it does not, they either reject the evidence as misleading or develop another hypothesis and go through the same procedure again. Decision analysts call this a satisficing strategy. (See Chapter 4, Strategies for Analytical Judgment.) Satisficing means picking the first solution that seems satisfactory, rather than going through all the possibilities to identify the very best solution. There may be several seemingly satisfactory solutions, but there is only one best solution.

Chapter 4 discussed the weaknesses in this approach. The principal concern is that if analysts focus mainly on trying to confirm one hypothesis they think is probably true, they can easily be led astray by the fact that there is so much evidence to support their point of view. They fail to recognize that most of this evidence is also consistent with other explanations or conclusions, and that these other alternatives have not been refuted.

Simultaneous evaluation of multiple, competing hypotheses is very difficult to do. To retain three to five or even seven hypotheses in working memory and note how each item of information fits into each hypothesis is beyond the mental capabilities of most people. It takes far greater mental agility than listing evidence supporting a single hypothesis that was pre-judged as the most likely answer. It can be accomplished, though, with the help of the simple procedures discussed here. The box below contains a step-by-step outline of the ACH process.

STEP 1

Identify the possible hypotheses to be considered. Use a group of analysts with different perspectives to brainstorm the possibilities.

Psychological research into how people go about generating hypotheses shows that people are actually rather poor at thinking of all the possibilities.[85] If a person does not even generate the correct hypothesis for consideration, obviously he or she will not get the correct answer.

Step-by-Step Outline of Analysis of Competing Hypotheses

1.   Identify the possible hypotheses to be considered. Use a group of analysts with different perspectives to brainstorm the possibilities.

2. Make a list of significant evidence and arguments for and against each hypothesis.

3. Prepare a matrix with hypotheses across the top and evidence down the side. Analyze the "diagnosticity" of the evidence and arguments--that is, identify which items are most helpful in judging the relative likelihood of the hypotheses.

4. Refine the matrix. Reconsider the hypotheses and delete evidence and arguments that have no diagnostic value.

5. Draw tentative conclusions about the relative likelihood of each hypothesis. Proceed by trying to disprove the hypotheses rather than prove them.

6. Analyze how sensitive your conclusion is to a few critical items of evidence. Consider the consequences for your analysis if that evidence were wrong, misleading, or subject to a different interpretation.

7. Report conclusions. Discuss the relative likelihood of all the hypotheses, not just the most likely one.

8. Identify milestones for future observation that may indicate events are taking a different course than expected.

It is useful to make a clear distinction between the hypothesis generation and hypothesis evaluation stages of analysis. Step 1 of the recommended analytical process is to identify all hypotheses that merit detailed examination. At this early hypothesis generation stage, it is very useful to bring together a group of analysts with different backgrounds and perspectives. Brainstorming in a group stimulates the imagination and may bring out possibilities that individual members of the group had not thought of. Initial discussion in the group should elicit every possibility, no matter how remote, before judging likelihood or feasibility. Only when all the possibilities are on the table should you then focus on judging them and selecting the hypotheses to be examined in greater detail in subsequent analysis.

When screening out the seemingly improbable hypotheses that you do not want to waste time on, it is necessary to distinguish hypotheses that appear to be *disproved* from those that are simply *unproven*. For an unproven hypothesis, there is no evidence that it is correct. For a disproved hypothesis, there is positive evidence that it is wrong. As discussed in Chapter 4, "Strategies for Analytical Judgment," and under Step 5 below, you should seek evidence that *disproves* hypotheses. Early rejection of unproven, but not disproved, hypotheses biases the subsequent analysis, because one does not then look for the evidence that might support them. Unproven hypotheses should be kept alive until they can be disproved.

One example of a hypothesis that often falls into this unproven but not disproved category is the hypothesis that an opponent is trying to deceive us. You may reject the possibility of denial and deception because you see no evidence of it, but rejection is not justified under these circumstances. If deception is planned well and properly implemented, one should not expect to find evidence of it readily at hand. The possibility should not be rejected until it is disproved, or, at least, until after a systematic search for evidence has been made and none has been found.

There is no "correct" number of hypotheses to be considered. The number depends upon the nature of the analytical problem and how advanced you are in the analysis of it. As a general rule, the greater your level of uncertainty, or the greater the policy impact of your conclusion, the more alternatives you may wish to consider. More than seven hypotheses may be unmanageable; if there are this many alternatives, it may be advisable to group several of them together for your initial cut at the analysis.

STEP 2

Make a list of significant evidence and arguments for and against each hypothesis.

In assembling the list of relevant evidence and arguments, these terms should be interpreted very broadly. They refer to all the factors that have an impact on your judgments about the hypotheses. Do not limit yourself to concrete evidence in the current intelligence reporting. Also include your own assumptions or logical deductions about another person's or group's or country's intentions, goals, or standard procedures. These assumptions may generate strong preconceptions as to which hypothesis is most likely. Such assumptions often drive your final judgment, so it is important to include them in the list of "evidence."

First, list the general evidence that applies to all the hypotheses. Then consider each hypothesis individually, listing factors that tend to support or contradict each one. You will commonly find that each hypothesis leads you to ask different questions and, therefore, to seek out somewhat different evidence.

For each hypothesis, ask yourself this question: If this hypothesis is true, what should I expect to be seeing or not seeing? What are all the things that must have happened, or may still be happening, and that one should expect to see evidence of? If you are not seeing this evidence, why not? Is it because it has not happened, it is not normally observable, it is being concealed from you, or because you or the intelligence collectors have not looked for it?

Note the absence of evidence as well as its presence. For example, when weighing the possibility of military attack by an adversary, the steps the adversary has not taken to ready his forces for attack may be more significant than the observable steps that have been taken. This recalls the Sherlock Holmes story in which the vital clue was that the dog did *not* bark in the night. One's attention tends to focus on what is reported rather than what is not reported. It requires a conscious effort to think about what is missing but should be present if a given hypothesis were true.

STEP 3

Prepare a matrix with hypotheses across the top and evidence down the side. Analyze the "diagnosticity" of the evidence and arguments- that is, identify which items are most helpful in judging the relative likelihood of alternative hypotheses.

Step 3 is perhaps the most important element of this analytical procedure. It is also the step that differs most from the natural, intuitive approach to analysis, and, therefore, the step you are most likely to overlook or misunderstand.

The procedure for Step 3 is to take the hypotheses from Step 1 and the evidence and arguments from Step 2 and put this information into a matrix format, with the hypotheses across the top and evidence and arguments down the side. This gives an overview of all the significant components of your analytical problem.

Then analyze how each piece of evidence relates to each hypothesis. This differs from the normal procedure, which is to look at one hypothesis at a time in order to consider how well the evidence supports that hypothesis. That will be done later, in Step 5. At this point, in Step 3, take one item of evidence at a time, then consider how consistent that evidence is with each of the hypotheses. Here is how to remember this distinction. In Step 3, you work *across* the rows of the matrix, examining one item of evidence at a time to see how consistent that item of evidence is with each of the hypotheses. In Step 5, you work *down* the columns of the matrix, examining one hypothesis at a time, to see how consistent that hypothesis is with all the evidence.

To fill in the matrix, take the first item of evidence and ask whether it is consistent with, inconsistent with, or irrelevant to each hypothesis. Then make a notation accordingly in the appropriate cell under each hypothesis in the matrix. The form of these notations in the matrix is a matter of personal preference. It may be pluses, minuses, and question marks. It may be C, I, and N/A standing for consistent, inconsistent, or not applicable. Or it may be some textual notation. In any event, it will be a simplification, a shorthand representation of the complex reasoning that went on as you thought about how the evidence relates to each hypothesis.

Hypotheses:
H1 - Iraq will not retaliate.
H2 - It will sponsor some minor terrorist actions.
H3 - Iraq is planning a major terrorist attack, perhaps against one or more CIA installations.

	H1	H2	H3
E1. Saddam public statement of intent not to retaliate.	+	+	+
E2. Absence of terrorist offensive during the 1991 Gulf War.	+	+	−
E3. Assumption that Iraq would not want to provoke another US attack.	+	+	−
E4. Increase in frequency/length of monitored Iraqi agent radio broadcasts.	−	+	+
E5. Iraqi embassies instructed to take increased security precautions.	−	+	+
E6. Assumption that failure to retaliate would be unacceptable loss of face for Saddam.	− −	+	+

Figure 15 Question: Will Iraq Retaliate for US Bombing of Its Intelligence Headquarters

After doing this for the first item of evidence, then go on to the next item of evidence and repeat the process until all cells in the matrix are filled. Figure 15 shows an example of how such a matrix might look. It uses as an example the intelligence question that arose after the US bombing of Iraqi intelligence headquarters in 1993: Will Iraq retaliate? The evidence in the matrix and how it is evaluated are hypothetical, fabricated for the purpose of providing a plausible example of the procedure. The matrix does not reflect actual evidence or judgments available at that time to the US Intelligence Community.

The matrix format helps you weigh the *diagnosticity* of each item of evidence, which is a key difference between analysis of competing hypotheses and traditional analysis. Diagnosticity of evidence is an important concept that is, unfortunately, unfamiliar to many analysts. It was introduced in Chapter 4, and that discussion is repeated here for your convenience.

Diagnosticity may be illustrated by a medical analogy. A high-temperature reading may have great value in telling a doctor that a patient is sick, but relatively little value in determining which illness a person is suffering from. Because a high temperature is consistent with so many possible hypotheses about a patient's illness, this evidence has limited diagnostic value in determining which illness (hypothesis) is the more likely one.

Evidence is diagnostic when it influences your judgment on the *relative* likelihood of the various hypotheses identified in Step 1. If an item of evidence seems consistent with all the hypotheses, it may have no diagnostic value. A common experience is to discover that most of the evidence supporting what you believe is the most likely hypothesis really is not very helpful, because that same evidence is also consistent with other hypotheses. When you do identify items that are highly diagnostic, these should drive your judgment. These are also the items for which you should re-check accuracy and consider alternative interpretations, as discussed in Step 6.

In the hypothetical matrix dealing with Iraqi intentions, note that evidence designated "E1" is assessed as consistent with all of the hypotheses. In other words, it has no diagnostic value. This is because we did not give any credence to Saddam's public statement on this question. He might say he will not retaliate but then do so, or state that he will retaliate and then not do it. On the other hand, E4 is diagnostic: increased frequency or length of Iraqi agent radio broadcasts is more likely to be observed if the Iraqis are planning retaliation than if they are not. The double minus for E6 indicates this is considered a very strong argument against H1. It is a linchpin assumption that drives the conclusion in favor of either H2 or H3. Several of the judgments reflected in this matrix will be questioned at a later stage in this analysis.

In some cases it may be useful to refine this procedure by using a numerical probability, rather than a general notation such as plus or minus, to describe how the evidence relates to each hypothesis. To do this, ask the following question for each cell in the matrix: If this hypothesis is true, what is the probability that I would be seeing this item of evidence? You may also make one or more additional notations in each cell of the matrix, such as:

- Adding a scale to show the intrinsic importance of each item of evidence.
- Adding a scale to show the ease with which items of evidence could be concealed, manipulated, or faked, or the extent to which one party might have an incentive to do so. This may be appropriate when the possibility of denial and deception is a serious issue.

STEP 4

Refine the matrix. Reconsider the hypotheses and delete evidence and arguments that have no diagnostic value.

The exact wording of the hypotheses is obviously critical to the conclusions one can draw from the analysis. By this point, you will have seen how the evidence breaks out under each hypothesis, and it will often be appropriate to reconsider and reword the hypotheses. Are there hypotheses that need to be added, or finer distinctions that need to be made in order to consider all the significant alternatives? If there is little orno evidence that helps distinguish between two hypotheses, should they be combined into one?

Also reconsider the evidence. Is your thinking about which hypotheses are most likely and least likely influenced by factors that are not included in the listing of evidence? If so, put them in. Delete from the matrix items of evidence or assumptions that now seem unimportant or have no diagnostic value. Save these items in a separate list as a record of information that was considered.

STEP 5

Draw tentative conclusions about the relative likelihood of each hypothesis. Proceed by trying to disprove hypotheses rather than prove them.

In Step 3, you worked across the matrix, focusing on a single item of evidence or argument and examining how it relates to each hypothesis. Now, work down the matrix, looking at each hypothesis as a whole. The matrix format gives an overview of all the evidence for and against all the hypotheses, so that you can examine all the hypotheses together and have them compete against each other for your favor.

In evaluating the relative likelihood of alternative hypotheses, start by looking for evidence or logical deductions that enable you to reject hypotheses, or at least to determine that they are unlikely. A fundamental precept of the scientific method is to proceed by rejecting or eliminating hypotheses, while tentatively accepting only those hypotheses that cannot be refuted. The scientific method obviously cannot be applied *in toto* to intuitive judgment, but the principle of seeking to disprove hypotheses, rather than confirm them, is useful.

No matter how much information is consistent with a given hypothesis, one cannot prove that hypothesis is true, because the same information may also be consistent with one or more other hypotheses. On the other hand, a single item of evidence that is inconsistent with a hypothesis may be sufficient grounds for rejecting that hypothesis. This was discussed in detail in Chapter 4, "Strategies for Analytical Judgment."

People have a natural tendency to concentrate on confirming hypotheses they already believe to be true, and they commonly give more weight to information that supports a hypothesis than to information that weakens it. This is wrong; we should do just the opposite. Step 5 again requires doing the *opposite* of what comes naturally.

In examining the matrix, look at the minuses, or whatever other notation you used to indicate evidence that may be inconsistent with a hypothesis. The hypotheses with the fewest minuses is probably the most likely one. The hypothesis with the most minuses is probably the least likely one. The fact that a hypothesis is inconsistent with the evidence is certainly a sound basis for rejecting it. The pluses, indicating evidence that is consistent with a hypothesis, are far less significant. It does not follow that the hypothesis with the most pluses is the most likely one, because a long list of evidence that is consistent with almost any reasonable hypothesis can be easily made. What is difficult to find, and is most significant when found, is hard evidence that is clearly inconsistent with a reasonable hypothesis.

This initial ranking by number of minuses is only a rough ranking, however, as some evidence obviously is more important than other evidence, and degrees of inconsistency cannot be captured by a single notation such as a plus or minus. By reconsidering the exact nature of the relationship between the evidence and the hypotheses, you will be able to judge how much weight to give it.

Analysts who follow this procedure often realize that their judgments are actually based on very few factors rather than on the large mass of information they thought was influencing their views. Chapter 5, "Do You Really Need More Information?," makes this same point based on experimental evidence.

The matrix should *not* dictate the conclusion to you. Rather, it should accurately reflect your judgment of what is important and how these important factors relate to the probability of each hypothesis. You, not the matrix, must make the decision. The matrix serves only as an aid to thinking and analysis, to ensure consideration of all the possible interrelationships between evidence and hypotheses and identification of those few items that really swing your judgment on the issue.

When the matrix shows that a given hypothesis is probable or unlikely, you may disagree. If so, it is because you omitted from the matrix one or more factors that have an important influence on your thinking. Go back and put them in, so that the analysis reflects your best judgment. If following this procedure has caused you to consider things you might otherwise have overlooked, or has caused you to revise your earlier estimate of the relative probabilities of the hypotheses, then the procedure has served a useful purpose. When you are done, the matrix serves as a shorthand record of your thinking and as an audit trail showing how you arrived at your conclusion.

This procedure forces you to spend more analytical time than you otherwise would on what you had thought were the less likely hypotheses. This is desirable. The seemingly less likely hypotheses usually involve plowing new ground and, therefore, require more work. What you started out thinking was the most likely hypothesis tends to be based on a continuation of your own past thinking. A principal advantage of the analysis of competing hypotheses is that it forces you to give a fairer shake to all the alternatives.

STEP 6

Analyze how sensitive your conclusion is to a few critical items of evidence. Consider the consequences for your analysis if that evidence were wrong, misleading, or subject to a different interpretation.

In Step 3 you identified the evidence and arguments that were most diagnostic, and in Step 5 you used these findings to make tentative judgments about the hypotheses. Now, go back and question the few linchpin assumptions or items of evidence that really drive the outcome of your analysis in one direction or the other. Are there questionable assumptions that underlie your understanding and interpretation? Are there alternative explanations or interpretations? Could the evidence be incomplete and, therefore, misleading?

If there is any concern at all about denial and deception, this is an appropriate place to consider that possibility. Look at the sources of your key evidence. Are any of the sources known to the authorities in the foreign country? Could the information have been manipulated? Put yourself in the shoes of a foreign deception planner to evaluate motive, opportunity, means, costs, and benefits of deception as they might appear to the foreign country.

When analysis turns out to be wrong, it is often because of key assumptions that went unchallenged and proved invalid. It is a truism that analysts should identify and question assumptions, but this is much easier said than done. The problem is to determine which assumptions merit questioning. One advantage of the ACH procedure is that it tells you what needs to be rechecked.

In Step 6 you may decide that additional research is needed to check key judgments. For example, it may be appropriate to go back to check original source materials rather than relying on someone else's interpretation. In writing your report, it is desirable to identify critical assumptions that went into your interpretation and to note that your conclusion is dependent upon the validity of these assumptions.

STEP 7

Report conclusions. Discuss the relative likelihood of all the hypotheses, not just the most likely one.

If your report is to be used as the basis for decisionmaking, it will be helpful for the decisionmaker to know the relative likelihood of all the alternative possibilities. Analytical judgments are never certain. There is always a good possibility of their being wrong. Decisionmakers need to make decisions on the basis of a full set of alternative possibilities, not just the single most likely alternative. Contingency or fallback plans may be needed in case one of the less likely alternatives turns out to be true.

If you say that a certain hypothesis is probably true, that could mean anywhere from a 55-percent to an 85-percent chance that future events will prove it correct. That leaves anywhere from a 15-percent to 45 percent possibility that a decision based on your judgment will be based on faulty assumptions and will turn out wrong. Can you be more specific about how confident you are in your judgment? Chapter 12, "Biases in Estimating Probabilities," discusses the difference between such "subjective probability" judgments and statistical probabilities based on data on relative frequencies.

When one recognizes the importance of proceeding by eliminating rather than confirming hypotheses, it becomes apparent that any written argument for a certain judgment is incomplete unless it also discusses alternative judgments that were considered and why they were rejected. In the past, at least, this was seldom done.

The narrative essay, which is the dominant art form for the presentation of intelligence judgments, does not lend itself to comparative evaluation of competing hypotheses. Consideration of alternatives adds to the length of reports and is perceived by many analysts as detracting from the persuasiveness of argument for the judgment chosen. Analysts may fear that the reader could fasten on one of the rejected alternatives as a good idea. Discussion of alternative hypotheses is nonetheless an important part of any intelligence appraisal, and ways can and should be found to include it.

STEP 8

Identify milestones for future observation that may indicate events are taking a different course than expected.

Analytical conclusions should always be regarded as tentative. The situation may change, or it may remain unchanged while you receive new information that alters your appraisal. It is always helpful to specify in advance things one should look for or be alert to that, if observed, would suggest a significant change in the probabilities. This is useful for intelligence consumers who are following the situation on a continuing basis. Specifying in advance what would cause you to change your mind will also make it more difficult for you to rationalize such developments, if they occur, as not really requiring any modification of your judgment.

SUMMARY AND CONCLUSION

Three key elements distinguish analysis of competing hypotheses from conventional intuitive analysis.

- Analysis starts with a full set of alternative possibilities, rather than with a most likely alternative for which the analyst seeks confirmation. This ensures that alternative hypotheses receive equal treatment and a fair shake.

- Analysis identifies and emphasizes the few items of evidence or assumptions that have the greatest diagnostic value in judging the relative likelihood of the alternative hypotheses. In conventional intuitive analysis, the fact that key evidence may also be consistent with alternative hypotheses is rarely considered explicitly and often ignored.

- Analysis of competing hypotheses involves seeking evidence to refute hypotheses. The most probable hypothesis is usually the one with the least evidence against it, not the one with the most evidence for it. Conventional analysis generally entails looking for evidence to confirm a favored hypothesis.

The analytical effectiveness of this procedure becomes apparent when considering the Indian nuclear weapons testing in 1998. According to Admiral Jeremiah, the Intelligence Community had reported that " there was no indication the Indians would test in the near term."[86] Such a conclusion by the Community would fail to distinguish an unproven hypothesis from a disproved hypothesis. An absence of evidence does not necessarily disprove the hypothesis that India will indeed test nuclear weapons.

If the ACH procedure had been used, one of the hypotheses would certainly have been that India is planning to test in the near term but will conceal preparations for the testing to forestall international pressure to halt such preparations.

Careful consideration of this alternative hypothesis would have required evaluating India's motive, opportunity, and means for concealing its intention until it was too late for the US and others to intervene. It would also have required assessing the ability of US intelligence to see through Indian denial and deception if it were being employed. It is hard to imagine that this would not have elevated awareness of the possibility of successful Indian deception.

A principal lesson is this. Whenever an intelligence analyst is tempted to write the phrase "there is no evidence that ...," the analyst should ask this question: If this hypothesis is true, can I realistically expect to see evidence of it? In other words, if India were planning nuclear tests while deliberately concealing its intentions, could the analyst realistically expect to see evidence of test planning? The ACH procedure leads the analyst to identify and face these kinds of questions.

Once you have gained practice in applying analysis of competing hypotheses, it is quite possible to integrate the basic concepts of this procedure into your normal analytical thought process. In that case, the entire eight-step procedure may be unnecessary, except on highly controversial issues.

There is no guarantee that ACH or any other procedure will produce a correct answer. The result, after all, still depends on fallible intuitive judgment applied to incomplete and ambiguous information. **Analysis of competing hypotheses does, however, guarantee an appropriate *process of analysis.* *This procedure leads you through a rational, systematic process that avoids some common analytical pitfalls. It increases the odds of getting the right answer, and it leaves an audit trail showing the evidence used in your analysis and how this evidence was interpreted. If others disagree with your judgment, the matrix can be used to highlight the precise area of disagreement. Subsequent discussion can then focus productively on the ultimate source of the differences.***

A common experience is that analysis of competing hypotheses attributes greater likelihood to alternative hypotheses than would conventional analysis. One becomes less confident of what one thought one knew. In focusing more attention on alternative explanations, the procedure brings out the full uncertainty inherent in any situation that is poor in data but rich in possibilities. Although such uncertainty is frustrating, it may be an accurate reflection of the true situation. As Voltaire said, "Doubt is not a pleasant state, but certainty is a ridiculous one."[87]

The ACH procedure has the offsetting advantage of focusing attention on the few items of critical evidence that cause the uncertainty or which, if they were available, would alleviate it. This can guide future collection, research, and analysis to resolve the uncertainty and produce a more accurate judgment.

PART III:
COGNITIVE BIASES

Chapter 9

WHAT ARE COGNITIVE BIASES?

SUMMARY

This mini-chapter discusses the nature of cognitive biases in general. The four chapters that follow it describe specific cognitive biases in the evaluation of evidence, perception of cause and effect, estimation of probabilities, and evaluation of intelligence reporting.

Fundamental limitations in human mental processes were identified in Chapters 2 and 3. A substantial body of research in cognitive psychology and decisionmaking is based on the premise that these cognitive limitations cause people to employ various simplifying strategies and rules of thumb to ease the burden of mentally processing information to make judgments and decisions.[88] These simple rules of thumb are often useful in helping us deal with complexity and ambiguity. Under many circumstances, however, they lead to predictably faulty judgments known as cognitive biases.

Cognitive biases are mental errors caused by our simplified information processing strategies. It is important to distinguish cognitive biases from other forms of bias, such as cultural bias, organizational bias, or bias that results from one's own self-interest. In other words, a cognitive bias does not result from any emotional or intellectual predisposition toward a certain judgment, but rather from subconscious mental procedures for processing information. A cognitive bias is a mental error that is consistent and predictable. For example:

The apparent distance of an object is determined in part by its clarity. The more sharply the object is seen, the closer it appears to be. This rule has some validity, because in any given scene the more distant objects are seen less sharply than nearer objects. However, the reliance on this rule leads to systematic errors in estimation of distance. Specifically, distances are often overestimated when visibility is poor because the contours of objects are blurred. On the other hand, distances are often underestimated when visibility is good because the objects are seen sharply. Thus the reliance on clarity as an indication of distance leads to common biases.[89]

This rule of thumb about judging distance is very useful. It usually works and helps us deal with the ambiguity and complexity of life around us. Under certain predictable circumstances, however, it will lead to biased judgment.

Cognitive biases are similar to optical illusions in that the error remains compelling even when one is fully aware of its nature. Awareness of the bias, by itself, does not produce a more accurate perception. Cognitive biases, therefore, are, exceedingly difficult to overcome.

Psychologists have conducted many experiments to identify the simplifying rules of thumb that people use to make judgments on incomplete or ambiguous information, and to show--at least in laboratory situations-- how these rules of thumb prejudice judgments and decisions. The following four chapters discuss cognitive biases that are particularly pertinent to intelligence analysis because they affect the evaluation of evidence, perception of cause and effect, estimation of probabilities, and retrospective evaluation of intelligence reports.

Before discussing the specific biases, it is appropriate to consider the nature of such experimental evidence and the extent to which one can generalize from these experiments to conclude that the same biases are prevalent in the Intelligence Community.

When psychological experiments reveal the existence of a bias, this does not mean that every judgment by every individual person will be biased. It means that in any group of people, the bias will exist to a greater or lesser degree in most judgments made by most of the group. On the basis of this kind of experimental evidence, one can only generalize about the tendencies of groups of people, not make statements about how any specific individual will think.

I believe that conclusions based on these laboratory experiments can be generalized to apply to intelligence analysts. In most, although not all cases, the test subjects were experts in their field. They were physicians, stock market analysts, horserace handicappers, chess masters, research directors, and professional psychologists, not undergraduate students as in so many psychological experiments. In most cases, the mental tasks performed in these experiments were realistic; that is, they were comparable to the judgments that specialists in these fields are normally required to make.

Some margin for error always exists when extrapolating from experimental laboratory to real-world experience, but classes of CIA analysts to whom these ideas were presented found them relevant and enlightening. I replicated a number of the simpler experiments with military officers in the National Security Affairs Department of the Naval Postgraduate School.

Chapter 10

BIASES IN EVALUATION OF EVIDENCE

SUMMARY

Evaluation of evidence is a crucial step in analysis, but what evidence people rely on and how they interpret it are influenced by a variety of extraneous factors. Information presented in vivid and concrete detail often has unwarranted impact, and people tend to disregard abstract or statistical information that may have greater evidential value. We seldom take the absence of evidence into account. The human mind is also oversensitive to the consistency of the evidence, and insufficiently sensitive to the reliability of the evidence. Finally, impressions often remain even after the evidence on which they are based has been totally discredited.[90]

The intelligence analyst works in a somewhat unique informational environment. Evidence comes from an unusually diverse set of sources: newspapers and wire services, observations by American Embassy officers, reports from controlled agents and casual informants, information exchanges with foreign governments, photo reconnaissance, and communications intelligence. Each source has its own unique strengths, weaknesses, potential or actual biases, and vulnerability to manipulation and deception. The most salient characteristic of the information environment is its diversity--multiple sources, each with varying degrees of reliability, and each commonly reporting information which by itself is incomplete and sometimes inconsistent or even incompatible with reporting from other sources. Conflicting information of uncertain reliability is endemic to intelligence analysis, as is the need to make rapid judgments on current events even before all the evidence is in.

The analyst has only limited control over the stream of information. Tasking of sources to report on specific subjects is often a cumbersome and time-consuming process. Evidence on some important topics is sporadic or nonexistent. Most human-source information is second hand at best.

Recognizing and avoiding biases under such circumstances is particularly difficult. Most of the biases discussed in this chapter are unrelated to each other and are grouped together here only because they all concern some aspect of the evaluation of evidence.

THE VIVIDNESS CRITERION

The impact of information on the human mind is only imperfectly related to its true value as evidence.[91] Specifically, information that is vivid, concrete, and personal has a greater impact on our thinking than pallid, abstract information that may actually have substantially greater value as evidence. For example:

- Information that people perceive directly, that they hear with their own ears or see with their own eyes, is likely to have greater impact than information received secondhand that may have greater evidential value.
- Case histories and anecdotes will have greater impact than more informative but abstract aggregate or statistical data.

Events that people experience personally are more memorable than those they only read about. Concrete words are easier to remember than abstract words,[92] and words of all types are easier to recall than numbers. In short, information having the qualities cited in the preceding paragraph is more likely to attract and hold our attention. It is more likely to be stored and remembered than abstract reasoning or statistical summaries, and therefore can be expected to have a greater immediate effect as well as a continuing impact on our thinking in the future.

Intelligence analysts generally work with secondhand information. The information that analysts receive is mediated by the written words of others rather than perceived directly with their own eyes and ears. Partly because of limitations imposed by their open CIA employment, many intelligence analysts have spent less time in the country they are analyzing and had fewer contacts with nationals of that country than their academic and other government colleagues. Occasions when an analyst does visit the country whose affairs he or she is analyzing, or speaks directly with a national from that country, are memorable experiences. Such experiences are often a source of new insights, but they can also be deceptive.

That concrete, sensory data do and should enjoy a certain priority when weighing evidence is well established. When an abstract theory or secondhand report is contradicted by personal observation, the latter properly prevails under most circumstances. There are a number of popular adages that advise mistrust of secondhand data: "Don't believe everything you read," "You can prove anything with statistics," "Seeing is believing," "I'm from Missouri..."

It is curious that there are no comparable maxims to warn against being misled by our own observations. Seeing should not always be believing.

Personal observations by intelligence analysts and agents can be as deceptive as secondhand accounts. Most individuals visiting foreign countries become familiar with only a small sample of people representing a narrow segment of the total society. Incomplete and distorted perceptions are a common result.

A familiar form of this error is the single, vivid case that outweighs a much larger body of statistical evidence or conclusions reached by abstract reasoning. When a potential car buyer overhears a stranger complaining about how his Volvo turned out to be a lemon, this may have as much impact on the potential buyer's thinking as statistics in *Consumer Reports* on the average annual repair costs for foreign-made cars. If the personal testimony comes from the potential buyer's brother or close friend, it will probably be given even more weight. Yet the logical status of this new information is to increase by one the sample on which the *Consumer Reports* statistics were based; the personal experience of a single Volvo owner has little evidential value.

Nisbett and Ross label this the "man-who" syndrome and provide the following illustrations:[93]

- "But I know a *man who* smoked three packs of cigarettes a day and lived to be ninety-nine."
- "I've never been to Turkey but just last month I met a *man who* had, and he found it . . ."

Needless to say, a "man-who" example seldom merits the evidential weight intended by the person citing the example, or the weight often accorded to it by the recipient.

The most serious implication of vividness as a criterion that determines the impact of evidence is that certain kinds of very valuable evidence will have little influence simply because they are abstract. Statistical data, in particular, lack the rich and concrete detail to evoke vivid images, and they are often overlooked, ignored, or minimized.

For example, the Surgeon General's report linking cigarette smoking to cancer should have, logically, caused a decline in per-capita cigarette consumption. No such decline occurred for more than 20 years. The reaction of physicians was particularly informative. All doctors were aware of the statistical evidence and were more exposed than the general population to the health problems caused by smoking. How they reacted to this evidence depended upon their medical specialty. Twenty years after the Surgeon General's report, radiologists who examine lung x-rays every day had the lowest rate of smoking. Physicians who diagnosed and treated lung cancer victims were also quite unlikely to smoke. Many other types of physicians continued to smoke. The probability that a physician continued to smoke was directly related to the distance of the physician's specialty from the lungs. In other words, even physicians, who were well qualified to understand and appreciate the statistical data, were more influenced by their vivid personal experiences than by valid statistical data.[94]

Personal anecdotes, actual accounts of people's responsiveness or indifference to information sources, and controlled experiments can all be cited *ad infinitum* "to illustrate the proposition that data summaries, despite their logically compelling implications, have less impact than does inferior but more vivid evidence."[95] It seems likely that intelligence analysts, too, assign insufficient weight to statistical information.

Analysts should give little weight to anecdotes and personal case histories unless they are known to be typical, and perhaps no weight at all if aggregate data based on a more valid sample can be obtained.

ABSENCE OF EVIDENCE

A principal characteristic of intelligence analysis is that key information is often lacking. Analytical problems are selected on the basis of their importance and the perceived needs of the consumers, without much regard for availability of information. Analysts have to do the best they can with what they have, somehow taking into account the fact that much relevant information is known to be missing.

Ideally, intelligence analysts should be able to recognize what relevant evidence is lacking and factor this into their calculations. They should also be able to estimate the potential impact of the missing data and to adjust confidence in their judgment accordingly. Unfortunately, this ideal does not appear to be the norm. Experiments suggest that "out of sight, out of mind" is a better description of the impact of gaps in the evidence.

This problem has been demonstrated using fault trees, which are schematic drawings showing all the things that might go wrong with any endeavor. Fault trees are often used to study the fallibility of complex systems such as a nuclear reactor or space capsule.

A fault tree showing all the reasons why a car might not start was shown to several groups of experienced mechanics.[96] The tree had seven major branches--insufficient battery charge, defective starting system, defective ignition system, defective fuel system, other engine problems, mischievous acts or vandalism, and all other problems--and a number of subcategories under each branch. One group was shown the full tree and asked to imagine 100 cases in which a car won't start. Members of this group were then asked to estimate how many of the 100 cases were attributable to each of the seven major branches of the tree. A second group of mechanics was shown only an incomplete version of the tree: three major branches were omitted in order to test how sensitive the test subjects were to what was left out.

If the mechanics' judgment had been fully sensitive to the missing information, then the number of cases of failure that would normally be attributed to the omitted branches should have been added to the "Other Problems" category. In practice, however, the "Other Problems" category was increased only half as much as it should have been. This indicated that the mechanics shown the incomplete tree were unable to fully recognize and incorporate into their judgments the fact that some of the causes for a car not starting were missing. When the same experiment was run with non-mechanics, the effect of the missing branches was much greater.

As compared with most questions of intelligence analysis, the "car won't start" experiment involved rather simple analytical judgments based on information that was presented in a well-organized manner. That the presentation of relevant variables in the abbreviated fault tree was incomplete could and should have been recognized by the experienced mechanics selected as test subjects. Intelligence analysts often have similar problems. Missing data is normal in intelligence problems, but it is probably more difficult to recognize that important information is absent and to incorporate this fact into judgments on intelligence questions than in the more concrete "car won't start" experiment.

As an antidote for this problem, analysts should identify explicitly those relevant variables on which information is lacking, consider alternative hypotheses concerning the status of these variables, and then modify their judgment and especially confidence in their judgment accordingly. They should also consider whether the absence of information is normal or is itself an indicator of unusual activity or inactivity.

OVERSENSITIVITY TO CONSISTENCY

The internal consistency in a pattern of evidence helps determine our confidence in judgments based on that evidence.[97] In one sense, consistency is clearly an appropriate guideline for evaluating evidence. People formulate alternative explanations or estimates and select the one that encompasses the greatest amount of evidence within a logically consistent scenario. Under some circumstances, however, consistency can be deceptive. Information may be consistent only because it is highly correlated or redundant, in which case many related reports may be no more informative than a single report. Or it may be consistent only because information is drawn from a very small sample or a biased sample.

Such problems are most likely to arise in intelligence analysis when analysts have little information, say on political attitudes of Russian military officers or among certain African ethnic groups. If the available evidence is consistent, analysts will often overlook the fact that it represents a very small and hence unreliable sample taken from a large and heterogeneous group. This is not simply a matter of necessity--of having to work with the information on hand, however imperfect it may be. Rather, there is an illusion of validity caused by the consistency of the information.

The tendency to place too much reliance on small samples has been dubbed the "law of small numbers."[98] This is a parody on the law of large numbers, the basic statistical principle that says very large samples will be highly representative of the population from which they are drawn. This is the principle that underlies opinion polling, but most people are not good intuitive statisticians. People do not have much intuitive feel for how large a sample has to be before they can draw valid conclusions from it. The so-called law of small numbers means that, intuitively, we make the mistake of treating small samples as though they were large ones.

This has been shown to be true even for mathematical psychologists with extensive training in statistics. Psychologists designing experiments have seriously incorrect notions about the amount of error and unreliability inherent in small samples of data, unwarranted confidence in the early trends from the first few data points, and unreasonably high expectations of being able to repeat the same experiment and get the same results with a different set of test subjects.

Are intelligence analysts also overly confident of conclusions drawn from very little data--especially if the data seem to be consistent? When working with a small but consistent body of evidence, analysts need to consider how representative that evidence is of the total body of potentially available information. If more reporting were available, how likely is it that this information, too, would be consistent with the already available evidence? If an analyst is stuck with only a small amount of evidence and cannot determine how representative this evidence is, confidence in judgments based on this evidence should be low regardless of the consistency of the information.

COPING WITH EVIDENCE OF UNCERTAIN ACCURACY

There are many reasons why information often is less than perfectly accurate: misunderstanding, misperception, or having only part of the story; bias on the part of the ultimate source; distortion in the reporting chain from subsource through source, case officer, reports officer, to analyst; or misunderstanding and misperception by the analyst. Further, much of the evidence analysts bring to bear in conducting analysis is retrieved from memory, but analysts often cannot remember even the source of information they have in memory let alone the degree of certainty they attributed to the accuracy of that information when it was first received.

The human mind has difficulty coping with complicated probabilistic relationships, so people tend to employ simple rules of thumb that reduce the burden of processing such information. In processing information of uncertain accuracy or reliability, analysts tend to make a simple yes or no decision. If they reject the evidence, they tend to reject it fully, so it plays no further role in their mental calculations. If they accept the evidence, they tend to accept it wholly, ignoring the probabilistic nature of the accuracy or reliability judgment. This is called a "best guess" strategy.[99] Such a strategy simplifies the integration of probabilistic information, but at the expense of ignoring some of the uncertainty. If analysts have information about which they are 70- or 80-percent certain but treat this information as though it were 100-percent certain, judgments based on that information will be overconfident.

A more sophisticated strategy is to make a judgment based on an assumption that the available evidence is perfectly accurate and reliable, then reduce the confidence in this judgment by a factor determined by the assessed validity of the information. For example, available evidence may indicate that an event probably (75 percent) will occur, but the analyst cannot be certain that the evidence on which this judgment is based is wholly accurate or reliable. Therefore, the analyst reduces the assessed probability of the event (say, down to 60 percent) to take into account the uncertainty concerning the evidence. This is an improvement over the best-guess strategy but generally still results in judgments that are overconfident when compared with the mathematical formula for calculating probabilities.[100]

In mathematical terms, the joint probability of two events is equal to the product of their individual probabilities. Imagine a situation in which you receive a report on event X that is probably (75 percent) true. *If the report on event X is true,* you judge that event Y will probably (75 percent) happen. The actual probability of Y is only 56 percent, which is derived by multiplying 75 percent times 75 percent.

In practice, life is not nearly so simple. Analysts must consider many items of evidence with different degrees of accuracy and reliability that are related in complex ways with varying degrees of probability to several potential outcomes. Clearly, one cannot make neat mathematical calculations that take all of these probabilistic relationships into account. In making intuitive judgments, we unconsciously seek shortcuts for sorting through this maze, and these shortcuts involve some degree of ignoring the uncertainty inherent in less-than-perfectly-reliable information. There seems to be little an analyst can do about this, short of breaking the analytical problem down in a way that permits assigning probabilities to individual items of information, and then using a mathematical formula to integrate these separate probability judgments.

The same processes may also affect our reaction to information that is plausible but known from the beginning to be of questionable authenticity. Ostensibly private statements by foreign officials are often reported though intelligence channels. In many instances it is not clear whether such a private statement by a foreign ambassador, cabinet member, or other official is an actual statement of private views, an indiscretion, part of a deliberate attempt to deceive the US Government, or part of an approved plan to convey a truthful message that the foreign government believes is best transmitted through informal channels.

The analyst who receives such a report often has little basis for judging the source's motivation, so the information must be judged on its own merits.

In making such an assessment, the analyst is influenced by plausible causal linkages. If these are linkages of which the analyst was already aware, the report has little impact inasmuch as it simply supports existing views. If there are plausible new linkages, however, thinking is restructured to take these into account. It seems likely that the impact on the analyst's thinking is determined solely by the substance of the information, and that the caveat concerning the source does not attenuate the impact of the information at all. Knowing that the information comes from an uncontrolled source who may be trying to manipulate us does not necessarily reduce the impact of the information.

PERSISTENCE OF IMPRESSIONS BASED ON DISCREDITED EVIDENCE

Impressions tend to persist even after the evidence that created those impressions has been fully discredited. Psychologists have become interested in this phenomenon because many of their experiments require that the test subjects be deceived. For example, test subjects may be made to believe they were successful or unsuccessful in performing some task, or that they possess certain abilities or personality traits, when this is not in fact the case. Professional ethics require that test subjects be disabused of these false impressions at the end of the experiment, but this has proved surprisingly difficult to achieve.

Test subjects' erroneous impressions concerning their logical problem-solving abilities persevered even after they were informed that manipulation of good or poor teaching performance had virtually guaranteed their success or failure.[101] Similarly, test subjects asked to distinguish true from fictitious suicide notes were given feedback that had no relationship to actual performance. The test subjects had been randomly divided into two groups, with members of one group being given the impression of above-average success and the other of relative failure at this task. The subjects' erroneous impressions of the difficulty of the task and of their own performance persisted even after they were informed of the deception--that is, informed that their alleged performance had been preordained by their assignment to one or the other test group. Moreover, the same phenomenon was found among observers of the experiment as well as the immediate participants.[102]

There are several cognitive processes that might account for this phenomenon. The tendency to interpret new information in the context of pre-existing impressions is relevant but probably not sufficient to explain why the pre-existing impression cannot be eradicated even when new information authoritatively discredits the evidence on which it is based.

An interesting but speculative explanation is based on the strong tendency to seek causal explanations, as discussed in the next chapter. When evidence is first received, people postulate a set of causal connections that explains this evidence. In the experiment with suicide notes, for example, one test subject attributed her apparent success in distinguishing real from fictitious notes to her empathetic personality and the insights she gained from the writings of a novelist who committed suicide. Another ascribed her apparent failure to lack of familiarity with people who might contemplate suicide. The stronger the perceived causal linkage, the stronger the impression created by the evidence.

Even after learning that the feedback concerning their performance was invalid, these subjects retained this plausible basis for inferring that they were either well or poorly qualified for the task. The previously perceived causal explanation of their ability or lack of ability still came easily to mind, independently of the now-discredited evidence that first brought it to mind.[103] Colloquially, one might say that once information rings a bell, the bell cannot be unrung.

The ambiguity of most real-world situations contributes to the operation of this perseverance phenomenon. Rarely in the real world is evidence so thoroughly discredited as is possible in the experimental laboratory. Imagine, for example, that you are told that a clandestine source who has been providing information for some time is actually under hostile control. Imagine further that you have formed a number of impressions on the basis of reporting from this source. It is easy to rationalize maintaining these impressions by arguing that the information was true despite the source being under control, or by doubting the validity of the report claiming the source to be under control. In the latter case, the perseverance of the impression may itself affect evaluation of the evidence that supposedly discredits the impression.

Chapter 11

BIASES IN PERCEPTION
OF CAUSE AND EFFECT

SUMMARY

Judgments about cause and effect are necessary to explain the past, understand the present, and estimate the future. These judgments are often biased by factors over which people exercise little conscious control, and this can influence many types of judgments made by intelligence analysts. Because of a need to impose order on our environment, we seek and often believe we find causes for what are actually accidental or random phenomena. People overestimate the extent to which other countries are pursuing a coherent, coordinated, rational plan, and thus also overestimate their own ability to predict future events in those nations. People also tend to assume that causes are similar to their effects, in the sense that important or large effects must have large causes.

When inferring the causes of behavior, too much weight is accorded to personal qualities and dispositions of the actor and not enough to situational determinants of the actor's behavior. People also overestimate their own importance as both a cause and a target of the behavior of others. Finally, people often perceive relationships that do not in fact exist, because they do not have an intuitive understanding of the kinds and amount of information needed to prove a relationship.

We cannot see cause and effect in the same sense that we see a desk or a tree. Even when we observe one billiard ball striking another and then watch the previously stationary ball begin to move, we are not perceiving cause and effect. The conclusion that one ball *caused* the other to move results only from a complex process of inference, not from direct sensory perception. That inference is based on the juxtaposition of events in time and space plus some theory or logical explanation as to why this happens.

There are several modes of analysis by which one might infer cause and effect. In more formal analysis, inferences are made through procedures that collectively comprise the scientific method. The scientist advances a hypothesis, then tests this hypothesis by the collection and statistical analysis of data on many instances of the phenomenon in question. Even then, causality cannot be proved beyond all possible doubt. The scientist seeks to disprove a hypothesis, not to confirm it. A hypothesis is accepted only when it cannot be rejected.

Collection of data on many comparable cases to test hypotheses about cause and effect is not feasible for most questions of interest to the Intelligence Community, especially questions of broad political or strategic import relating to another country's intentions. To be sure, it is feasible more often than it is done, and increased use of scientific procedures in political, economic, and strategic research is much to be encouraged. But the fact remains that the dominant approach to intelligence analysis is necessarily quite different. It is the approach of the historian rather than the scientist, and this approach presents obstacles to accurate inferences about causality.

The procedures and criteria most historians use to attribute causality are less well defined than the scientist's.

> The historian's aim [is] to make a coherent whole out of the events he studies. His way of doing that, I suggest, is to look for certain dominant concepts or leading ideas by which to illuminate his facts, to trace the connections between those ideas themselves, and then to show how the detailed facts became intelligible in the light of them by constructing a "significant" narrative of the events of the period in question.[104]

The key ideas here are coherence and narrative. These are the principles that guide the organization of observations into meaningful structures and patterns. The historian commonly observes only a single case, not a pattern of covariation (when two things are related so that change in one is associated with change in the other) in many comparable cases. Moreover, the historian observes simultaneous changes in so many variables that the principle of covariation generally is not helpful in sorting out the complex relationships among them. The narrative story, on the other hand, offers a means of organizing the rich complexity of the historian's observations. The historian uses imagination to construct a coherent story out of fragments of data.

The intelligence analyst employing the historical mode of analysis is essentially a storyteller. He or she constructs a plot from the previous events, and this plot then dictates the possible endings of the incomplete story. The plot is formed of the "dominant concepts or leading ideas" that the analyst uses to postulate patterns of relationships among the available data. The analyst is not, of course, preparing a work of fiction. There are constraints on the analyst's imagination, but imagination is nonetheless involved because there is an almost unlimited variety of ways in which the available data might be organized to tell a meaningful story. The constraints are the available evidence and the principle of coherence. The story must form a logical and coherent whole and be internally consistent as well as consistent with the available evidence.

Recognizing that the historical or narrative mode of analysis involves telling a coherent story helps explain the many disagreements among analysts, inasmuch as coherence is a subjective concept. It assumes some prior beliefs or mental model about what goes with what. More relevant to this discussion, the use of coherence rather than scientific observation as the criterion for judging truth leads to biases that presumably influence all analysts to some degree. Judgments of coherence may be influenced by many extraneous factors, and if analysts tend to favor certain types of explanations as more coherent than others, they will be biased in favor of those explanations.

BIAS IN FAVOR OF CAUSAL EXPLANATIONS

One bias attributable to the search for coherence is a tendency to favor causal explanations. Coherence implies order, so people naturally arrange observations into regular patterns and relationships. If no pattern is apparent, our first thought is that we lack understanding, not that we are dealing with random phenomena that have no purpose or reason. As a last resort, many people attribute happenings that they cannot understand to God's will or to fate, which is somehow preordained; they resist the thought that outcomes may be determined by forces that interact in random, unpredictable ways. People generally do not accept the notion of chance or randomness. Even dice players behave as though they exert some control over the outcome of a throw of dice.[105] The prevalence of the word "because" in everyday language reflects the human tendency to seek to identify causes.

People expect patterned events to look patterned, and random events to look random, but this is not the case. Random events often look patterned.

The random process of flipping a coin six times may result in six consecutive heads. Of the 32 possible sequences resulting from six coin flips, few actually look "random."[106] This is because randomness is a property of the process that generates the data that are produced. Randomness may in some cases be demonstrated by scientific (statistical) analysis. However, events will almost never be perceived intuitively as being random; one can find an apparent pattern in almost any set of data or create a coherent narrative from any set of events.

Because of a need to impose order on their environment, people seek and often believe they find causes for what are actually random phenomena. During World War II, Londoners advanced a variety of causal explanations for the pattern of German bombing. Such explanations frequently guided their decisions about where to live and when to take refuge in air raid shelters. Postwar examination, however, determined that the clustering of bomb hits was close to a random distribution.[107]

The Germans presumably intended a purposeful pattern, but purposes changed over time and they were not always achieved, so the net result was an almost random pattern of bomb hits. Londoners focused their attention on the few clusters of hits that supported their hypotheses concerning German intentions--not on the many cases that did not.

Some research in paleobiology seems to illustrate the same tendency. A group of paleobiologists has developed a computer program to simulate evolutionary changes in animal species over time. But the transitions from one time period to the next are not determined by natural selection or any other regular process: they are determined by computer-generated random numbers. The patterns produced by this program are similar to the patterns in nature that paleobiologists have been trying to understand. Hypothetical evolutionary events that seem, intuitively, to have a strong pattern were, in fact, generated by random processes.[108]

Yet another example of imposing causal explanations on random events is taken from a study dealing with the research practices of psychologists. When experimental results deviated from expectations, these scientists rarely attributed the deviation to variance in the sample. They were always able to come up with a more persuasive causal explanation for the discrepancy.[109]

B. F. Skinner even noted a similar phenomenon in the course of experiments with the behavioral conditioning of pigeons. The normal pattern of these experiments was that the pigeons were given positive reinforcement, in the form of food, whenever they pecked on the proper lever at the proper time. To obtain the food regularly, they had to learn to peck in a certain sequence. Skinner demonstrated that the pigeons "learned" and followed a pattern (which Skinner termed a superstition) even when the food was actually dispensed randomly.[110]

These examples suggest that in military and foreign affairs, where the patterns are at best difficult to fathom, there may be many events for which there are no valid causal explanations. This certainly affects the predictability of events and suggests limitations on what might logically be expected of intelligence analysts.

BIAS FAVORING PERCEPTION
OF CENTRALIZED DIRECTION

Very similar to the bias toward causal explanations is a tendency to see the actions of other governments (or groups of any type) as the intentional result of centralized direction and planning. "...most people are slow to perceive accidents, unintended consequences, coincidences, and small causes leading to large effects. Instead, coordinated actions, plans and conspiracies are seen."[111] Analysts overestimate the extent to which other countries are pursuing coherent, rational, goal-maximizing policies, because this makes for more coherent, logical, rational explanations. This bias also leads analysts and policymakers alike to overestimate the predictability of future events in other countries.

Analysts know that outcomes are often caused by accident, blunder, coincidence, the unintended consequence of well-intentioned policy, improperly executed orders, bargaining among semi-independent bureaucratic entities, or following standard operating procedures under inappropriate circumstances.[112] But a focus on such causes implies a disorderly world in which outcomes are determined more by chance than purpose. It is especially difficult to incorporate these random and usually unpredictable elements into a coherent narrative, because evidence is seldom available to document them on a timely basis. It is only in historical perspective, after memoirs are written and government documents released, that the full story becomes available.

This bias has important consequences. Assuming that a foreign government's actions result from a logical and centrally directed plan leads an analyst to:

- Have expectations regarding that government's actions that may not be fulfilled if the behavior is actually the product of shifting or

inconsistent values, bureaucratic bargaining, or sheer confusion and
blunder.

- Draw far-reaching but possibly unwarranted inferences from
  isolated statements or actions by government officials who may be
  acting on their own rather than on central direction.
- Overestimate the United States' ability to influence the other
  government's actions.
- Perceive inconsistent policies as the result of duplicity and
  Machiavellian maneuvers, rather than as the product of weak
  leadership, vacillation, or bargaining among diverse bureaucratic or
  political interests.

SIMILARITY OF CAUSE AND EFFECT

When systematic analysis of covariation is not feasible and several
alternative causal explanations seem possible, one rule of thumb people use
to make judgments of cause and effect is to consider the similarity between
attributes of the cause and attributes of the effect. Properties of the cause are
"...inferred on the basis of being correspondent with or similar to properties
of the effect."[113] Heavy things make heavy noises; dainty things move
daintily; large animals leave large tracks. When dealing with physical
properties, such inferences are generally correct.

People tend, however, to reason in the same way under circumstances
when this inference is not valid. Thus, analysts tend to assume that economic
events have primarily economic causes, that big events have important
consequences, and that little events cannot affect the course of history. Such
correspondence between cause and effect makes a more logical and
persuasive--a more coherent--narrative, but there is little basis for expecting
such inferences to correspond to historical fact.

Fischer labels the assumption that a cause must somehow resemble its
effect the "fallacy of identity,"[114] and he cites as an example the
historiography of the Spanish Armada. Over a period of several centuries,
historians have written of the important consequences of the English defeat
of the Spanish Armada in 1588. After refuting each of these arguments,
Fischer notes:

In short, it appears that the defeat of the Armada, mighty and
melodramatic as it was, may have been remarkably barren of result. Its
defeat may have caused very little, except the disruption of the Spanish
strategy that sent it on its way. That judgment is sure to violate the patriotic

instincts of every Englishman and the aesthetic sensibilities of us all. A big event *must* have big results, we think.[115]

The tendency to reason according to similarity of cause and effect is frequently found in conjunction with the previously noted bias toward inferring centralized direction. Together, they explain the persuasiveness of conspiracy theories. Such theories are invoked to explain large effects for which there do not otherwise appear to be correspondingly large causes. For example, it seems "...outrageous that a single, pathetic, weak figure like Lee Harvey Oswald should alter world history."[116] Because the purported motive for the assassination of John Kennedy is so dissimilar from the effect it is alleged to explain, in the minds of many it fails to meet the criterion of a coherent narrative explanation. If such "little" causes as mistakes, accidents, or the aberrant behavior of a single individual have big effects, then the implication follows that major events happen for reasons that are senseless and random rather than by purposeful direction.

Intelligence analysts are more exposed than most people to hard evidence of real plots, coups, and conspiracies in the international arena. Despite this--or perhaps because of it--most intelligence analysts are not especially prone to what are generally regarded as conspiracy theories. Although analysts may not exhibit this bias in such extreme form, the bias presumably does influence analytical judgments in myriad little ways. In examining causal relationships, analysts generally construct causal explanations that are somehow commensurate with the magnitude of their effects and that attribute events to human purposes or predictable forces rather than to human weakness, confusion, or unintended consequences.

INTERNAL VS. EXTERNAL CAUSES OF BEHAVIOR

Much research into how people assess the causes of behavior employs a basic dichotomy between internal determinants and external determinants of human actions. Internal causes of behavior include a person's attitudes, beliefs, and personality. External causes include incentives and constraints, role requirements, social pressures, or other forces over which the individual has little control. The research examines the circumstances under which people attribute behavior either to stable dispositions of the actor or to characteristics of the situation to which the actor responds.

Differences in judgments about what causes another person's or government's behavior affect how people respond to that behavior. How people respond to friendly or unfriendly actions by others may be quite different if they attribute the behavior to the nature of the person or government than if they see the behavior as resulting from situational constraints over which the person or government has little control.

A fundamental error made in judging the causes of behavior is to overestimate the role of internal factors and underestimate the role of external factors. When observing another's behavior, people are too inclined to infer that the behavior was caused by broad personal qualities or dispositions of the other person and to expect that these same inherent qualities will determine the actor's behavior under other circumstances. Not enough weight is assigned to external circumstances that may have influenced the other person's choice of behavior. This pervasive tendency has been demonstrated in many experiments under quite diverse circumstances[117] and has often been observed in diplomatic and military interactions.[118]

Susceptibility to this biased attribution of causality depends upon whether people are examining their own behavior or observing that of others. It is the behavior of others that people tend to attribute to the nature of the actor, whereas they see their own behavior as conditioned almost entirely by the situation in which they find themselves. This difference is explained largely by differences in information available to actors and observers. People know a lot more about themselves.

The actor has a detailed awareness of the history of his or her own actions under similar circumstances. In assessing the causes of our own behavior, we are likely to consider our previous behavior and focus on how it has been influenced by different situations. Thus situational variables become the basis for explaining our own behavior. This contrasts with the observer, who typically lacks this detailed knowledge of the other person's past behavior. The observer is inclined to focus on how the other person's behavior compares with the behavior of others under similar circumstances.[119] This difference in the type and amount of information available to actors and observers applies to governments as well as people.

An actor's personal involvement with the actions being observed enhances the likelihood of bias. "Where the observer is also an actor, he is likely to exaggerate the uniqueness and emphasize the dispositional origins of the responses of others to his own actions."[120] This is because the observer assumes his or her own actions are unprovocative, clearly understood by other actors, and well designed to elicit a desired response. Indeed, an observer interacting with another actor sees himself as determining the situation to which the other actor responds. When the actor does not respond as expected, the logical inference is that the response was caused by the nature of the actor rather than by the nature of the situation.

Intelligence analysts are familiar with the problem of weighing internal versus external causes of behavior in a number of contexts. When a new leader assumes control of a foreign government, analysts assess the likely impact of changed leadership on government policy. For example, will the former Defense Minister who becomes Prime Minister continue to push for increases in the defense budget? Analysts weigh the known predispositions of the new Prime Minister, based on performance in previous positions, against the requirements of the situation that constrain the available options. If relatively complete information is available on the situational constraints, analysts may make an accurate judgment on such questions. Lacking such information, they tend to err on the side of assuming that the individual's personal predispositions will prompt continuation of past behavior.

Consider the Soviet invasion of Afghanistan. The Soviets' perception of their own behavior was undoubtedly very different from the American perception. Causal attribution theory suggests that Soviet leaders would see the invasion as a reaction to the imperatives of the situation in South Asia at that time, such as the threat of Islamic nationalism spreading from Iran and Afghanistan into the Soviet Union. Further, they would perceive US failure to understand their "legitimate" national interests as caused by fundamental US hostility.[121]

Conversely, observers of the Soviet invasion would be inclined to attribute it to the aggressive and expansionist nature of the Soviet regime. Dislike of the Soviet Union and lack of information on the situational constraints as perceived by the Soviets themselves would be likely to exacerbate the attributional bias.[122] Further, to the extent that this bias stemmed from insufficient knowledge of situational pressures and constraints, one might expect policymakers who were not Soviet experts to have had a stronger bias than analysts specializing in the Soviet Union. With their greater base of information on the situational variables, the specialists may be better able to take these variables into account.

Specialists on occasion become so deeply immersed in the affairs of the country they are analyzing that they begin to assume the perspective--and the biases--of that country's leaders. During the Cold War, there was a persistent difference between CIA specialists in Soviet affairs and specialists in Chinese affairs when dealing with Sino-Soviet relations. During border clashes in 1969, for example, specialists on the USSR argued that the Chinese were being "provocative." These specialists tended to accept the Soviet regime's versions as to the history and alignment of the border.

Specialists in Chinese affairs tended to take the opposite view--that is, that the arrogant Russians were behaving like Russians often do, while the Chinese were simply reacting to the Soviet high-handedness.[123] In other words, the analysts assumed the same biased perspective as the leaders of the country about which they were most knowledgeable. An objective account of causal relationships might have been somewhere between these two positions.

The Egypt-Israel peace negotiations in 1978-1979 offered another example of apparent bias in causal attribution. In the words of one observer at the time:

> Egyptians attribute their willingness to sign a treaty with Israel as due to their inherent disposition for peace; Israelis explain Egyptian willingness to make peace as resulting from a deteriorating economy and a growing awareness of Israel's military superiority. On the other hand, Israelis attribute their own orientation for accommodation as being due to their ever-present preference for peace. Egypt, however, explains Israel's compromises regarding, for example, Sinai, as resulting from external pressures such as positive inducements and threats of negative sanctions by the United States. In addition, some Egyptians attribute Israel's undesirable behavior, such as establishment of Jewish settlements on the West Bank of the Jordan River, as stemming from Zionist expansionism. If Israel should not place settlements in that territory, Egyptians might account for such desirable behavior as being due to external constraints, such as Western condemnation of settlements. Israelis, on the other hand explain undesirable behavior, such as Egypt's past tendency to issue threats to drive them into the sea, as resulting from Egypt's inherent opposition to a Jewish state in the Middle East. When Egyptians ceased to make such threats, Israelis attributed this desirable behavior as emanating from external circumstances, such as Israel's relative military superiority.[124]

The persistent tendency to attribute cause and effect in this manner is not simply the consequence of self-interest or propaganda by the opposing sides. Rather, it is the readily understandable and predictable result of how people normally attribute causality under many different circumstances.

As a general rule, biased attribution of causality helps sow the seeds of mistrust and misunderstanding between people and between governments. We tend to have quite different perceptions of the causes of each other's behavior.

OVERESTIMATING OUR OWN IMPORTANCE

Individuals and governments tend to overestimate the extent to which they successfully influence the behavior of others.[125] This is an exception to the previously noted generalization that observers attribute the behavior of others to the nature of the actor. It occurs largely because a person is so familiar with his or her own efforts to influence another, but much less well informed about other factors that may have influenced the other's decision.

In estimating the influence of US policy on the actions of another government, analysts more often than not will be knowledgeable of US actions and what they are intended to achieve, but in many instances they will be less well informed concerning the internal processes, political pressures, policy conflicts, and other influences on the decision of the target government.

This bias may have played a role in the recent US failure to anticipate Indian nuclear weapons testing even though the new Indian Government was elected partly on promises it would add nuclear weapons to India's military arsenal. Most US intelligence analysts apparently discounted the promises as campaign rhetoric, believing that India would be dissuaded from joining the nuclear club by economic sanctions and diplomatic pressure. Analysts overestimated the ability of US policy to influence Indian decisions.

When another country's actions are consistent with US desires, the most obvious explanation, in the absence of strong evidence to the contrary, is that US policy effectively influenced the decision.[126] Conversely, when another country behaves in an undesired manner, this is normally attributed to factors beyond US control. People and governments seldom consider the possibility that their own actions have had unintended consequences. They assume that their intentions have been correctly perceived and that actions will have the desired effect unless frustrated by external causes.

Many surveys and laboratory experiments have shown that people generally perceive their own actions as the cause of their successes but not of their failures. When children or students or workers perform well, their parents, teachers, or supervisors take at least part of the credit; when they do poorly, their mentors seldom assume any blame. Successful candidates for Congress generally believe their own behavior contributed strongly to their victory, while unsuccessful candidates blame defeat on factors beyond their control.

Another example is the chest thumping that some Americans engaged in after the fall of the Soviet Union. According to some, the demise of the USSR was caused by strong US policies, such as increased defense expenditures and the Strategic Defense Initiative, which caused Soviet leaders to realize they could no longer compete with the United States. The US news media played this story for several weeks, interviewing many people--some experts, some not--on why the Soviet Union collapsed. Most serious students understood that there were many reasons for the Soviet collapse, the most important of which were internal problems caused by the nature of the Soviet system.

People and governments also tend to overestimate their own importance as the target of others' actions. They are sensitive to the impact that others' actions have on them, and they generally assume that people and governments intend to do what they do and intend it to have the effect that it has. They are much less aware of, and consequently tend to downgrade the importance of, other causes or results of the action.

In analyzing the reasons why others act the way they do, it is common to ask, "What goals are the person or government pursuing?" But goals are generally inferred from the effects of behavior, and the effects that are best known and often seem most important are the effects upon ourselves. Thus actions that hurt us are commonly interpreted as intentional expressions of hostility directed at ourselves. Of course, this will often be an accurate interpretation, but people sometimes fail to recognize that actions that seem directed at them are actually the unintended consequence of decisions made for other reasons.

ILLUSORY CORRELATION

At the start of this chapter, covariation was cited as one basis for inferring causality. It was noted that covariation may either be observed intuitively or measured statistically. This section examines the extent to which the intuitive perception of covariation deviates from the statistical measurement of covariation.

Statistical measurement of covariation is known as correlation. Two events are correlated when the existence of one event implies the existence of the other. Variables are correlated when a change in one variable implies a similar degree of change in another. Correlation alone does not necessarily imply causation. For example, two events might co-occur because they have a common cause, rather than because one causes the other. But when two events or changes do co-occur, and the time sequence is such that one always follows the other, people often infer that the first caused the second. Thus, inaccurate perception of correlation leads to inaccurate perception of cause and effect.

Judgments about correlation are fundamental to all intelligence analysis. For example, assumptions that worsening economic conditions lead to increased political support for an opposition party, that domestic problems may lead to foreign adventurism, that military government leads to unraveling of democratic institutions, or that negotiations are more successful when conducted from a position of strength are all based on intuitive judgments of correlation between these variables. In many cases these assumptions are correct, but they are seldom tested by systematic observation and statistical analysis.

Much intelligence analysis is based on common-sense assumptions about how people and governments normally behave. The problem is that people possess a great facility for invoking contradictory "laws" of behavior to explain, predict, or justify different actions occurring under similar circumstances. "Haste makes waste" and "He who hesitates is lost" are examples of inconsistent explanations and admonitions. They make great sense when used alone and leave us looking foolish when presented together. "Appeasement invites aggression" and "agreement is based upon compromise" are similarly contradictory expressions.

When confronted with such apparent contradictions, the natural defense is that "it all depends on. ..." Recognizing the need for such qualifying statements is one of the differences between subconscious information processing and systematic, self-conscious analysis. Knowledgeable analysis might be identified by the ability to fill in the qualification; careful analysis by the frequency with which one remembers to do so.[127]

Illusory correlation occurs when people perceive a relationship that does not in fact exist. In looking at a series of cases, it seems that people often focus on instances that support the existence of a relationship but ignore those cases that fail to support it. Several experiments have demonstrated that people do not have an intuitive understanding of what information is really needed to assess the relationship between two events or two variables. There appears to be nothing in people's intuitive understanding that corresponds with the statistical concept of correlation.

Nurses were tested on their ability to learn through experience to judge the relationship, or correlation, between a symptom and the diagnosis of illness.[128] The nurses were each shown 100 cards; every card ostensibly represented one patient. The cards had a row of four letters at the top representing various symptoms and another row of four letters at the bottom representing diagnoses. The nurses were instructed to focus on just one letter

(A) representing one symptom and one letter (F) representing one diagnosis, and then to judge whether the symptom A was related to the diagnosis F. In other words, on the basis of experience with these 100 "patients," does the presence of symptom A help to diagnose the presence of illness F? The experiment was run a number of times using different degrees of relationship between A and F.

Put yourself briefly in the position of a test subject. You have gone through the cards and noticed that on about 25 of them, or a quarter of the cases, the symptom and the disease, A and F, are both present. Would you say there is a relationship? Why? Is it appropriate to make a judgment solely on the basis of the frequency of cases which support the hypothesis of a relationship between A and F? What else do you need to know? Would it be helpful to have the number of cases in which the symptom (A) was present without the disease (F)? Let us say this was also true on 25 cards, so that out of the 100 cards, 50 had A and 25 of those cards with A also had F. In other words, the disease was present in half the cases in which the symptom was observed. Is this sufficient to establish a relationship, or is it also necessary to know the number of times the disease was present without the symptom?

Actually, to determine the existence of such a relationship, one needs information to fill all four cells of a 2 x 2 contingency table. Figure 16 shows such a table for one test run of this experiment. The table shows the number of cases of patients having each of four possible combinations of symptom and disease.

	A	Not A
F	25	25
Not F	25	25

Figure 16

Eighteen of 19 test subjects given the 100 cards representing this particular combination of A and F thought there was at least a weak relationship, and several thought there was a strong relationship, when in fact, there is no correlation at all. More than half the test subjects based their judgment solely on the frequency of cases in which both A and F were present. This is the upper left cell of the table. These subjects were trying to determine if there was a relationship between A and F. When looking through the cards, 25 percent of the cases they looked at were consistent with the belief that symptom and diagnosis were perfectly correlated; this appears to be a lot of evidence to support the hypothesized relationship. Another smaller group of test subjects used somewhat more sophisticated reasoning. They looked at the total number of A cases and then asked in how many of these cases F was also present. This is the left side of the table in Figure 16. A third group resisted the basic concept of making a statistical generalization. When asked to describe their reasoning, they said that sometimes a relationship was present while in other cases it was not.

Of the 86 test subjects involved in several runnings of this experiment, not a single one showed any intuitive understanding of the concept of correlation. That is, no one understood that to make a proper judgment about the existence of a relationship, one must have information on all four cells of the table. Statistical correlation in its most elementary form is based on the ratio of the sums of the frequencies in the diagonal cells of a 2 x 2 table. In other words, a predominance of entries along either diagonal represents a strong statistical relationship between the two variables.

Let us now consider a similar question of correlation on a topic of interest to intelligence analysts. What are the characteristics of strategic deception and how can analysts detect it? In studying deception, one of the important questions is: what are the correlates of deception? Historically, when analysts study instances of deception, what else do they see that goes along with it, that is somehow related to deception, and that might be interpret as an indicator of deception? Are there certain practices relating to deception, or circumstances under which deception is most likely to occur, that permit one to say, that, because we have seen x or y or z, this most likely means a deception plan is under way? This would be comparable to a doctor observing certain symptoms and concluding that a given disease may be present. This is essentially a problem of correlation. If one could identify several correlates of deception, this would significantly aid efforts to detect it.

The hypothesis has been advanced that deception is most likely when the stakes are exceptionally high.[129] If this hypothesis is correct, analysts should be especially alert for deception in such instances. One can cite prominent examples to support the hypothesis, such as Pearl Harbor, the Normandy landings, and the German invasion of the Soviet Union. It seems as though the hypothesis has considerable support, given that it is so easy to recall examples of high stakes situations in which deception was employed. But consider what it would take to prove, empirically, that such a relationship actually exists. Figure 17 sets up the problem as a 2 x 2 contingency table.

	High Stakes	Not High Stakes
Deception	68	?
No Deception	35	?

Figure 17

Barton Whaley researched 68 cases in which surprise or deception was present in strategic military operations between 1914 and 1968.[130] Let us assume that some form of deception, as well as surprise, was present in all 68 cases and put this number in the upper left cell of the table. How many cases are there with high stakes when deception was not used? That is a lot harder to think about and to find out about; researchers seldom devote much effort to documenting negative cases, when something did not occur. Fortunately, Whaley did make a rough estimate that both deception and surprise were absent in one-third to one-half of the cases of "grand strategy" during this period, which is the basis for putting the number 35 in the lower left cell of Figure 17.

How common is deception when the stakes are not high? This is the upper right cell of Figure 17. Entries for this cell and the lower right cell are difficult to estimate; they require defining a universe of cases that includes low-stakes situations. What is a low-stakes situation in this context? High-stakes situations are definable, but there is an almost infinite number and variety of low-stakes situations. Because of this difficulty, it may not be feasible to use the full 2 x 2 table to analyze the relationship between deception and high stakes.

Perhaps it is necessary to be content with only the left side of the Figure 17 table. But then we cannot demonstrate empirically that one should be more alert to deception in high-stakes situations, because there is no basis for comparing high-stakes and low-stakes cases. If deception is even more common in tactical situations than it is in high stakes strategic situations, then analysts should not be more inclined to suspect deception when the stakes are high.

It is not really clear whether there is a relationship between deception and high-stakes situations, because there are not enough data. Intuitively, your gut feeling may tell you there is, and this feeling may well be correct. But you may have this feeling mainly because you are inclined to focus only on those cases in the upper left cell that do suggest such a relationship. People tend to overlook cases where the relationship does not exist, inasmuch as these are much less salient.

The lesson to be learned is not that analysts should do a statistical analysis of every relationship. They usually will not have the data, time, or interest for that. But analysts should have a general understanding of what it takes to know whether a relationship exists. This understanding is definitely not a part of people's intuitive knowledge. It does not come naturally. It has to be learned. When dealing with such issues, analysts have to force themselves to think about all four cells of the table and the data that would be required to fill each cell.

Even if analysts follow these admonitions, there are several factors that distort judgment when one does not follow rigorous scientific procedures in making and recording observations. These are factors that influence a person's ability to recall examples that fit into the four cells. For example, people remember occurrences more readily than non-occurrences. "History is, by and large, a record of what people did, not what they failed to do."[131]

Thus, instances in which deception occurred are easier to recall than instances in which it did not. Analysts remember occurrences that support the relationship they are examining better than those that do not. To the extent that perception is influenced by expectations, analysts may have missed or discounted the contrary instances. People also have a better memory for recent events, events in which they were personally involved, events that had important consequences, and so forth. These factors have a significant influence on perceptions of correlation when analysts make a gut judgment without consciously trying to think of all four cells of the table.

Many erroneous theories are perpetuated because they seem plausible and because people record their experience in a way that supports rather than refutes them. Ross describes this process as follows:

> ...the intuitive observer selectively codes those data potentially relevant to the relationship between X and Y. Data points that fit his hypotheses and predictions are accepted as reliable, valid, representative, and free of error or "third-variable influences." Such data points are seen as reflective of the "real"...relationship between X and Y. By contrast, data points that deviate markedly from the intuitive ... expectations or theory are unlikely to be

given great weight and tend to be dismissed as unreliable, erroneous, unrepresentative, or the product of contaminating third-variable influences. Thus the intuitive scientist who believes that fat men are jolly, or more specifically that fatness causes jolliness, will see particular fat and jolly men as strong evidence for this theory; he will not entertain the hypothesis that an individual's jollity is mere pretense or the product of a particularly happy home life rather than obesity. By contrast, fat and morose individuals will be examined very carefully before gaining admission to that scientist's store of relevant data. He might, for instance, seek to determine whether the individual's moroseness on the day in question is atypical, or the result of a nagging cold or a disappointing day, rather than the reflection of some stable attribute. It need hardly be emphasized that even a randomly generated [set of data] can yield a relatively high correlation if coded in the manner just outlined.[132]

Chapter 12

BIASES IN ESTIMATING PROBABILITIES

SUMMARY

In making rough probability judgments, people commonly depend upon one of several simplified rules of thumb that greatly ease the burden of decision. Using the "availability" rule, people judge the probability of an event by the ease with which they can imagine relevant instances of similar events or the number of such events that they can easily remember. With the "anchoring" strategy, people pick some natural starting point for a first approximation and then adjust this figure based on the results of additional information or analysis. Typically, they do not adjust the initial judgment enough.

Expressions of probability, such as possible and probable, are a common source of ambiguity that make it easier for a reader to interpret a report as consistent with the reader's own preconceptions. The probability of a scenario is often miscalculated. Data on "prior probabilities" are commonly ignored unless they illuminate causal relationships.

AVAILABILITY RULE

One simplified rule of thumb commonly used in making probability estimates is known as the availability rule. In this context, "availability" refers to imaginability or retrievability from memory. Psychologists have shown that two cues people use unconsciously in judging the probability of an event are the ease with which they can imagine relevant instances of the event and the number or frequency of such events that they can easily remember.[133] People are using the availability rule of thumb whenever they estimate frequency or probability on the basis of how easily they can recall or imagine instances of whatever it is they are trying to estimate.

Normally this works quite well. If one thing actually occurs more frequently than another and is therefore more probable, we probably can recall more instances of it. Events that are likely to occur usually are easier to imagine than unlikely events. People are constantly making inferences based on these assumptions. For example, we estimate our chances for promotion by recalling instances of promotion among our colleagues in similar positions and with similar experience. We estimate the probability that a politician will lose an election by imagining ways in which he may lose popular support.

Although this often works well, people are frequently led astray when the ease with which things come to mind is influenced by factors unrelated to their probability. The ability to recall instances of an event is influenced by how recently the event occurred, whether we were personally involved, whether there were vivid and memorable details associated with the event, and how important it seemed at the time. These and other factors that influence judgment are unrelated to the true probability of an event.

Consider two people who are smokers. One had a father who died of lung cancer, whereas the other does not know anyone who ever had lung cancer. The one whose father died of lung cancer will normally perceive a greater probability of adverse health consequences associated with smoking, even though one more case of lung cancer is statistically insignificant when weighing such risk. How about two CIA officers, one of whom knew Aldrich Ames and the other who did not personally know anyone who had ever turned out to be a traitor? Which one is likely to perceive the greatest risk of insider betrayal?

It was difficult to imagine the breakup of the Soviet Union because such an event was so foreign to our experience of the previous 50 years. How difficult is it now to imagine a return to a Communist regime in Russia? Not so difficult, in part because we still have vivid memories of the old Soviet Union. But is that a sound basis for estimating the likelihood of its happening? When analysts make quick, gut judgments without really analyzing the situation, they are likely to be influenced by the availability bias. The more a prospective scenario accords with one's experience, the easier it is to imagine and the more likely it seems.

Intelligence analysts may be less influenced than others by the availability bias. Analysts are evaluating all available information, not making quick and easy inferences. On the other hand, policymakers and journalists who lack the time or access to evidence to go into details must necessarily take shortcuts. The obvious shortcut is to use the availability rule of thumb for making inferences about probability.

Many events of concern to intelligence analysts

> ...are perceived as so unique that past history does not seem relevant to the evaluation of their likelihood. In thinking of such events we often construct scenarios, i.e., stories that lead from the present situation to the target event. The plausibility of the scenarios that come to mind, or the difficulty of producing them, serve as clues to the likelihood of the event. If no reasonable scenario comes to mind, the event is deemed impossible or highly unlikely. If several scenarios come easily to mind, or if one scenario is particularly compelling, the event in question appears probable.[134]

US policymakers in the early years of our involvement in Vietnam had to imagine scenarios for what might happen if they did or did not commit US troops to the defense of South Vietnam. In judging the probability of alternative outcomes, our senior leaders were strongly influenced by the ready availability of two seemingly comparable scenarios--the failure of appeasement prior to World War II and the successful intervention in Korea.

Many extraneous factors influence the imaginability of scenarios for future events, just as they influence the retrievability of events from memory. Curiously, one of these is the act of analysis itself. The act of constructing a detailed scenario for a possible future event makes that event more readily imaginable and, therefore, increases its perceived probability. This is the experience of CIA analysts who have used various tradecraft tools that require, or are especially suited to, the analysis of unlikely but nonetheless possible and important hypotheses. (Such techniques were discussed in Chapter 6, "Keeping an Open Mind" and Chapter 8, "Analysis of Competing Hypotheses.") The analysis usually results in the "unlikely" scenario being taken a little more seriously. This phenomenon has also been demonstrated in psychological experiments.[135]

In sum, the availability rule of thumb is often used to make judgments about likelihood or frequency. People would be hard put to do otherwise, inasmuch as it is such a timesaver in the many instances when more detailed analysis is not warranted or not feasible. Intelligence analysts, however, need to be aware when they are taking shortcuts. They must know the strengths and weaknesses of these procedures, and be able to identify when they are most likely to be led astray. For intelligence analysts, recognition that they are employing the availability rule should raise a caution flag. Serious analysis of probability requires identification and assessment of the strength and interaction of the many variables that will determine the outcome of a situation.

ANCHORING

Another strategy people seem to use intuitively and unconsciously to simplify the task of making judgments is called anchoring. Some natural starting point, perhaps from a previous analysis of the same subject or from some partial calculation, is used as a first approximation to the desired judgment. This starting point is then adjusted, based on the results of additional information or analysis. Typically, however, the starting point serves as an anchor or drag that reduces the amount of adjustment, so the final estimate remains closer to the starting point than it ought to be.

Anchoring can be demonstrated very simply in a classroom exercise by asking a group of students to estimate one or more known quantities, such as the percentage of member countries in the United Nations that are located in Africa. Give half the students a low-percentage number and half a high-percentage number. Ask them to start with this number as an estimated answer, then, as they think about the problem, to adjust this number until they get as close as possible to what they believe is the correct answer. When this was done in one experiment that used this question, those starting with an anchor of 10 percent produced adjusted estimates that averaged 25 percent. Those who started with an anchor of 65 percent produced adjusted estimates that averaged 45 percent.[136]

Because of insufficient adjustment, those who started out with an estimate that was too high ended with significantly higher estimates than those who began with an estimate that was too low. Even the totally arbitrary starting points acted as anchors, causing drag or inertia that inhibited fulladjustment of estimates.

Whenever analysts move into a new analytical area and take over responsibility for updating a series of judgments or estimates made by their predecessors, the previous judgments may have such an anchoring effect. Even when analysts make their own initial judgment, and then attempt to revise this judgment on the basis of new information or further analysis, there is much evidence to suggest that they usually do not change the judgment enough.

Anchoring provides a partial explanation of experiments showing that analysts tend to be overly sure of themselves in setting confidence ranges. A military analyst who estimates future missile or tank production is often unable to give a specific figure as a point estimate. The analyst may, therefore, set a range from high to low, and estimate that there is, say, a 75-percent chance that the actual production figure will fall within this range. If a number of such estimates are made that reflect an appropriate degree of confidence, the true figure should fall within the estimated range 75 percent of the time and outside this range 25 percent of the time. In experimental situations, however, most participants are overconfident. The true figure falls outside the estimated range a much larger percentage of the time.[137]

If the estimated range is based on relatively hard information concerning the upper and lower limits, the estimate is likely to be accurate. If, however, the range is determined by starting with a single best estimate that is simply adjusted up and down to arrive at estimated maximum and minimum values, then anchoring comes into play, and the adjustment is likely to be insufficient.

Reasons for the anchoring phenomenon are not well understood. The initial estimate serves as a hook on which people hang their first impressions or the results of earlier calculations. In recalculating, they take this as a starting point rather than starting over from scratch, but why this should limit the range of subsequent reasoning is not clear.

There is some evidence that awareness of the anchoring problem is not an adequate antidote.[138] This is a common finding in experiments dealing with cognitive biases. The biases persist even after test subjects are informed of them and instructed to try to avoid them or compensate for them.

One technique for avoiding the anchoring bias, to weigh anchor so to speak, may be to ignore one's own or others' earlier judgments and rethink a problem from scratch. In other words, consciously avoid any prior judgment as a starting point. There is no experimental evidence to show that this is possible or that it will work, but it seems worth trying. Alternatively, it is sometimes possible to avoid human error by employing formal statistical procedures. Bayesian statistical analysis, for example, can be used to revise prior judgments on the basis of new information in a way that avoids anchoring bias.[139]

EXPRESSION OF UNCERTAINTY

Probabilities may be expressed in two ways. Statistical probabilities are based on empirical evidence concerning relative frequencies. Most intelligence judgments deal with one-of-a-kind situations for which it is impossible to assign a statistical probability. Another approach commonly used in intelligence analysis is to make a "subjective probability" or "personal probability" judgment. Such a judgment is an expression of the analyst's personal belief that a certain explanation or estimate is correct. It is comparable to a judgment that a horse has a three-to-one chance of winning a race.

Verbal expressions of uncertainty--such as "possible," "probable," "unlikely," "may," and "could"--are a form of subjective probability judgment, but they have long been recognized as sources of ambiguity and misunderstanding. To say that something could happen or is possible may refer to anything from a 1-percent to a 99-percent probability. To express themselves clearly, analysts must learn to routinely communicate uncertainty using the language of numerical probability or odds ratios.

As explained in Chapter 2 on "Perception," people tend to see what they expect to see, and new information is typically assimilated to existing beliefs. This is especially true when dealing with verbal expressions of uncertainty. By themselves, these expressions have no clear meaning. They are empty shells. The reader or listener fills them with meaning through the context in which they are used and what is already in the reader's or listener's mind about that context.

When intelligence conclusions are couched in ambiguous terms, a reader's interpretation of the conclusions will be biased in favor of consistency with what the reader already believes. This may be one reason why many intelligence consumers say they do not learn much from intelligence reports.[140]

It is easy to demonstrate this phenomenon in training courses for analysts. Give students a short intelligence report, have them underline all expressions of uncertainty, then have them express their understanding of the report by writing above each expression of uncertainty the numerical probability they believe was intended by the writer of the report. This is an excellent learning experience, as the differences among students in how they understand the report are typically so great as to be quite memorable.

In one experiment, an intelligence analyst was asked to substitute numerical probability estimates for the verbal qualifiers in one of his own earlier articles. The first statement was: "The cease-fire is holding but could be broken within a week." The analyst said he meant there was about a 30-percent chance the cease-fire would be broken within a week. Another analyst who had helped this analyst prepare the article said she thought there was about an 80-percent chance that the cease-fire would be broken. Yet, when working together on the report, both analysts had believed they were in agreement about what could happen.[141] Obviously, the analysts had not even communicated effectively with each other, let alone with the readers of their report.

Sherman Kent, the first director of CIA's Office of National Estimates, was one of the first to recognize problems of communication caused by imprecise statements of uncertainty. Unfortunately, several decades after Kent was first jolted by how policymakers interpreted the term "serious possibility" in a national estimate, this miscommunication between analysts and policymakers, and between analysts, is still a common occurrence.[142]

I personally recall an ongoing debate with a colleague over the bona fides of a very important source. I argued he was probably bona fide. My colleague contended that the source was probably under hostile control. After several months of periodic disagreement, I finally asked my colleague to put a number on it. He said there was at least a 51-percent chance of the source being under hostile control. I said there was at least a 51-percent chance of his being bona fide. Obviously, we agreed that there was a great deal of uncertainty. That stopped our disagreement. The problem was not a major difference of opinion, but the ambiguity of the term probable.

The table in Figure 18 shows the results of an experiment with 23 NATO military officers accustomed to reading intelligence reports. They were given a number of sentences such as: "It is highly unlikely that ...." All the sentences were the same except that the verbal expressions of probability changed. The officers were asked what percentage probability they would attribute to each statement if they read it in an intelligence report. Each dot in the table represents one officer's probability assignment.[143] While there was broad consensus about the meaning of "better than even," there was a wide disparity in interpretation of other probability expressions. The shaded areas in the table show the ranges proposed by Kent.[144]

The main point is that an intelligence report may have no impact on the reader if it is couched in such ambiguous language that the reader can easily interpret it as consistent with his or her own preconceptions. This ambiguity can be especially troubling when dealing with low-probability, high-impact dangers against which policymakers may wish to make contingency plans.

Consider, for example, a report that there is little chance of a terrorist attack against the American Embassy in Cairo at this time. If the Ambassador's preconception is that there is no more than a one-in-a-hundred chance, he may elect to not do very much. If the Ambassador's preconception is that there may be as much as a one-in-four chance of an attack, he may decide to do quite a bit. The term "little chance" is consistent with either of those interpretations, and there is no way to know what the report writer meant.

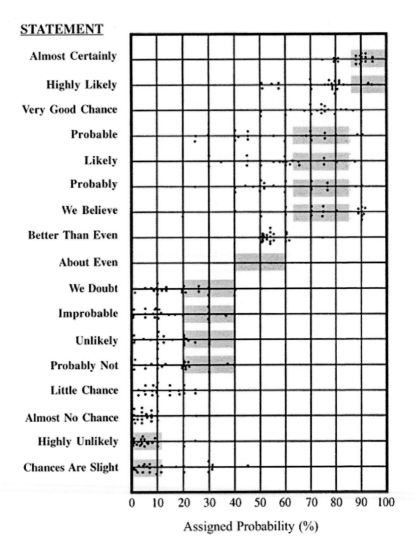

Figure 18. Measuring Perceptions of Uncertainty

Another potential ambiguity is the phrase "at this time." Shortening the time frame for prediction lowers the probability, but may not decrease the need for preventive measures or contingency planning. An event for which the timing is unpredictable may "at this time" have only a 5-percent probability of occurring during the coming month, but a 60-percent probability if the time frame is extended to one year (5 percent per month for 12 months).

How can analysts express uncertainty without being unclear about how certain they are? Putting a numerical qualifier in parentheses after the phrase expressing degree of uncertainty is an appropriate means of avoiding misinterpretation. This may be an odds ratio (less than a one-in-four chance) or a percentage range (5 to 20 percent) or (less than 20 percent). Odds ratios are often preferable, as most people have a better intuitive understanding of odds than of percentages.

ASSESSING PROBABILITY OF A SCENARIO

Intelligence analysts sometimes present judgments in the form of a scenario--a series of events leading to an anticipated outcome. There is evidence that judgments concerning the probability of a scenario are influenced by amount and nature of detail in the scenario in a way that is unrelated to actual likelihood of the scenario.

A scenario consists of several events linked together in a narrative description. To calculate mathematically the probability of a scenario, the proper procedure is to multiply the probabilities of each individual event. Thus, for a scenario with three events, each of which will probably (70 percent certainty) occur, the probability of the scenario is .70 x .70 x .70 or slightly over 34 percent. Adding a fourth probable (70 percent) event to the scenario would reduce its probability to 24 percent.

Most people do not have a good intuitive grasp of probabilistic reasoning. One approach to simplifying such problems is to assume (or think as though) one or more probable events have already occurred. This eliminates some of the uncertainty from the judgment. Another way to simplify the problem is to base judgment on a rough average of the probabilities of each event. In the above example, the averaging procedure gives an estimated probability of 70 percent for the entire scenario. Thus, the scenario appears far more likely than is in fact the case.

When the averaging strategy is employed, highly probable events in the scenario tend to offset less probable events. This violates the principle that a chain cannot be stronger than its weakest link. Mathematically, the least probable event in a scenario sets the upper limit on the probability of the scenario as a whole. If the averaging strategy is employed, additional details may be added to the scenario that are so plausible they increase the perceived

probability of the scenario, while, mathematically, additional events must
necessarily reduce its probability.[145]

Base-rate Fallacy

In assessing a situation, an analyst sometimes has two kinds of evidence
available--specific evidence about the individual case at hand, and numerical
data that summarize information about many similar cases. This type of
numerical information is called a base rate or prior probability. The base-rate
fallacy is that the numerical data are commonly ignored unless they
illuminate a causal relationship. This is illustrated by the following
experiment. [146]

During the Vietnam War, a fighter plane made a non-fatal strafing attack
on a US aerial reconnaissance mission at twilight. Both Cambodian and
Vietnamese jets operate in the area. You know the following facts:

a)   Specific case information: The US pilot identified the fighter as
     Cambodian. The pilot's aircraft recognition capabilities were tested
     under appropriate visibility and flight conditions. When presented
     with a sample of fighters (half with Vietnamese markings and half
     with Cambodian) the pilot made correct identifications 80 percent
     of the time and erred 20 percent of the time.

b)   Base rate data: 85 percent of the jet fighters in that area are
     Vietnamese; 15 percent are Cambodian.

Question: What is the probability that the fighter was Cambodian rather
than Vietnamese?

A common procedure in answering this question is to reason as follows:
We know the pilot identified the aircraft as Cambodian. We also know the
pilot's identifications are correct 80 percent of the time; therefore, there is an
80 percent probability the fighter was Cambodian. This reasoning appears
plausible but is incorrect. It ignores the base rate--that 85 percent of the
fighters in that area are Vietnamese. The base rate, or prior probability, is
what you can say about any hostile fighter in that area before you learn
anything about the specific sighting.

It is actually more likely that the plane was Vietnamese than Cambodian
despite the pilot's "probably correct" identification. Readers who are
unfamiliar with probabilistic reasoning and do not grasp this point should
imagine 100 cases in which the pilot has a similar encounter. Based on

paragraph (a), we know that 80 percent or 68 of the 85 Vietnamese aircraft will be correctly identified as Vietnamese, while 20 percent or 17 will be incorrectly identified as Cambodian. Based on paragraph (b), we know that 85 of these encounters will be with Vietnamese aircraft, 15 with Cambodian.

Similarly, 80 percent or 12 of the 15 Cambodian aircraft will be correctly identified as Cambodian, while 20 percent or three will be incorrectly identified as Vietnamese. This makes a total of 71 Vietnamese and 29 Cambodian sightings, of which only 12 of the 29 Cambodian sightings are correct; the other 17 are incorrect sightings of Vietnamese aircraft. Therefore, when the pilot claims the attack was by a Cambodian fighter, the probability that the craft was actually Cambodian is only 12/29ths or 41 percent, despite the fact that the pilot's identifications are correct 80 percent of the time.

This may seem like a mathematical trick, but it is not. The difference stems from the strong prior probability of the pilot observing a Vietnamese aircraft. The difficulty in understanding this arises because untrained intuitive judgment does not incorporate some of the basic statistical principles of probabilistic reasoning. Most people do not incorporate the prior probability into their reasoning because it does not seem relevant. It does not seem relevant because there is no causal relationship between the background information on the percentages of jet fighters in the area and the pilot's observation.[147] The fact that 85 percent of the fighters in the area were Vietnamese and 15 percent Cambodian did not *cause* the attack to be made by a Cambodian rather than a Vietnamese.

To appreciate the different impact made by causally relevant background information, consider this alternative formulation of the same problem. In paragraph (b) of the problem, substitute the following:

(b) Although the fighter forces of the two countries are roughly equal in number in this area, 85 percent of all harassment incidents involve Vietnamese fighters, while 15 percent involve Cambodian fighters.

The problem remains mathematically and structurally the same. Experiments with many test subjects, however, show it is quite different psychologically because it readily elicits a causal explanation relating the prior probabilities to the pilot's observation. If the Vietnamese have a propensity to harass and the Cambodians do not, the prior probability that Vietnamese harassment is more likely than Cambodian is no longer ignored.

Linking the prior probability to a cause and effect relationship immediately raises the possibility that the pilot's observation was in error.

With this revised formulation of the problem, most people are likely to reason as follows: We know from past experience in cases such as this that the harassment is usually done by Vietnamese aircraft. Yet, we have a fairly reliable report from our pilot that it was a Cambodian fighter. These two conflicting pieces of evidence cancel each other out. Therefore, we do not know--it is roughly 50-50 whether it was Cambodian or Vietnamese. In employing this reasoning, we use the prior probability information, integrate it with the case-specific information, and arrive at a conclusion that is about as close to the optimal answer (still 41 percent) as one is going to get without doing a mathematical calculation.

There are, of course, few problems in which base rates are given as explicitly as in the Vietnamese/Cambodian aircraft example. When base rates are not well known but must be inferred or researched, they are even less likely to be used.[148]

The so-called planning fallacy, to which I personally plead guilty, is an example of a problem in which base rates are not given in numerical terms but must be abstracted from experience. In planning a research project, I may estimate being able to complete it in four weeks. This estimate is based on relevant case-specific evidence: desired length of report, availability of source materials, difficulty of the subject matter, allowance for both predictable and unforeseeable interruptions, and so on. I also possess a body of experience with similar estimates I have made in the past. Like many others, I almost never complete a research project within the initially estimated time frame! But I am seduced by the immediacy and persuasiveness of the case-specific evidence. All the causally relevant evidence about the project indicates I should be able to complete the work in the time allotted for it. Even though I know from experience that this never happens, I do not learn from this experience. I continue to ignore the non-causal, probabilistic evidence based on many similar projects in the past, and to estimate completion dates that I hardly ever meet. (Preparation of this book took twice as long as I had anticipated. These biases are, indeed, difficult to avoid!)

Chapter 13

HINDSIGHT BIASES IN EVALUATION
OF INTELLIGENCE REPORTING

SUMMARY

Evaluations of intelligence analysis--analysts' own evaluations of their judgments as well as others' evaluations of intelligence products--are distorted by systematic biases. As a result, analysts overestimate the quality of their analytical performance, and others underestimate the value and quality of their efforts. These biases are not simply the product of self-interest and lack of objectivity. They stem from the nature of human mental processes and are difficult and perhaps impossible to overcome.[149]
Hindsight biases influence the evaluation of intelligence reporting in three ways:

- Analysts normally overestimate the accuracy of their past judgments.
- Intelligence consumers normally underestimate how much they learned from intelligence reports.
- Overseers of intelligence production who conduct postmortem analyses of an intelligence failure normally judge that events were more readily foreseeable than was in fact the case.

None of the biases is surprising. Analysts have observed these tendencies in others, although probably not in themselves. What may be unexpected is that these biases are not only the product of self-interest and lack of objectivity. They are examples of a broader phenomenon that is built into human mental processes and that cannot be overcome by the simple admonition to be more objective.

Psychologists who conducted the experiments described below tried to teach test subjects to overcome these biases. Experimental subjects with no vested interest in the results were briefed on the biases and encouraged to avoid them or compensate for them, but could not do so. Like optical illusions, cognitive biases remain compelling even after we become aware of them.

The analyst, consumer, and overseer evaluating analytical performance all have one thing in common. They are exercising hindsight. They take their current state of knowledge and compare it with what they or others did or could or should have known before the current knowledge was received. This is in sharp contrast with intelligence estimation, which is an exercise in foresight, and it is the difference between these two modes of thought--hindsight and foresight--that seems to be a source of bias.

The amount of good information that is available obviously is greater in hindsight than in foresight. There are several possible explanations of how this affects mental processes. One is that the additional information available for hindsight changes perceptions of a situation so naturally and so immediately that people are largely unaware of the change. When new information is received, it is immediately and unconsciously assimilated into our pre-existing knowledge. If this new information adds significantly to our knowledge--that is, if it tells the outcome of a situation or the answer to a question about which we were previously uncertain--our mental images are restructured to take the new information into account. With the benefit of hindsight, for example, factors previously considered relevant may become irrelevant, and factors previously thought to have little relevance may be seen as determinative.

After a view has been restructured to assimilate the new information, there is virtually no way to accurately reconstruct the pre-existing mental set. Once the bell has rung, it cannot be unrung. A person may *remember* his or her previous judgments if not much time has elapsed and the judgments were precisely articulated, but apparently people cannot accurately *reconstruct* their previous thinking. The effort to reconstruct what we previously thought about a given situation, or what we would have thought about it, is inevitably influenced by our current thought patterns. Knowing the outcome of a situation makes it harder to imagine other outcomes that might have been considered. Unfortunately, simply understanding that the mind works in this fashion does little to help overcome the limitation.

The overall message to be learned from an understanding of these biases, as shown in the experiments described below, is that an analyst's intelligence judgments are not as good as analysts think they are, or as bad as others seem to believe. Because the biases generally cannot be overcome, they would appear to be facts of life that analysts need to take into account in evaluating their own performance and in determining what evaluations to expect from others. This suggests the need for a more systematic effort to:

- Define what should be expected from intelligence analysts.
- Develop an institutionalized procedure for comparing intelligence judgments and estimates with actual outcomes.
- Measure how well analysts live up to the defined expectations.

The discussion now turns to the experimental evidence demonstrating these biases from the perspective of the analyst, consumer, and overseer of intelligence.

THE ANALYST'S PERSPECTIVE

Analysts interested in improving their own performance need to evaluate their past estimates in the light of subsequent developments. To do this, analysts must either remember (or be able to refer to) their past estimates or must reconstruct their past estimates on the basis of what they remember having known about the situation at the time the estimates were made. The effectiveness of the evaluation process, and of the learning process to which it gives impetus, depends in part upon the accuracy of these remembered or reconstructed estimates.

Experimental evidence suggests a systematic tendency toward faulty memory of past estimates.[150] That is, when events occur, people tend to overestimate the extent to which they had previously expected them to occur. And conversely, when events do not occur, people tend to underestimate the probability they had previously assigned to their occurrence. In short, events generally seem less surprising than they should on the basis of past estimates. This experimental evidence accords with analysts' intuitive experience. Analysts rarely appear--or allow themselves to appear--very surprised by the course of events they are following.

In experiments to test the bias in memory of past estimates, 119 subjects were asked to estimate the probability that a number of events would or would not occur during President Nixon's trips to Peking and Moscow in

1972. Fifteen possible outcomes were identified for each trip, and each subject assigned a probability to each of these outcomes. The outcomes were selected to cover the range of possible developments and to elicit a wide range of probability values.

At varying time periods after the trips, the same subjects were asked to remember or reconstruct their own predictions as accurately as possible. (No mention was made of the memory task at the time of the original prediction.) Then the subjects were asked to indicate whether they thought each event had or had not occurred during these trips.

When three to six months were allowed to elapse between the subjects' estimates and their recollection of these estimates, 84 percent of the subjects exhibited the bias when dealing with events they believed actually did happen. That is, the probabilities they remembered having estimated were higher than their actual estimates of events they believed actually did occur. Similarly, for events they believed did not occur, the probabilities they remembered having estimated were lower than their actual estimates, although here the bias was not as great. For both kinds of events, the bias was more pronounced after three to six months had elapsed than when subjects were asked to recall estimates they had given only two weeks earlier.

In summary, knowledge of the outcomes somehow affected most test subjects' memory of their previous estimates of these outcomes, and the more time that was allowed for memories to fade, the greater the effect of the bias. The developments during the President's trips were perceived as less surprising than they would have been if actual estimates were compared with actual outcomes. For the 84 percent of subjects who showed the anticipated bias, their retrospective evaluation of their estimative performance was clearly more favorable than warranted by the facts.

THE CONSUMER'S PERSPECTIVE

When consumers of intelligence reports evaluate the quality of the intelligence product, they ask themselves the question: "How much did I learn from these reports that I did not already know?" In answering this question, there is a consistent tendency for most people to underestimate the contribution made by new information. This "I knew it all along" bias causes consumers to undervalue the intelligence product.[151]

That people do in fact commonly react to new information in this manner was tested in a series of experiments involving some 320 people, each of whom answered the same set of 75 factual questions taken from almanacs and encyclopedias. As a measure of their confidence in their answers, the subjects assigned to each question a number ranging from 50 percent to 100 percent, indicating their estimate of the probability that they had chosen the correct answer.

As a second step in the experiment, subjects were divided into three groups. The first group was given 25 of the previously asked questions and instructed to respond to them exactly as they had previously. This simply tested the subjects' ability to remember their previous answers. The second group was given the same set of 25 questions but with the correct answers circled "for your [the subjects'] general information." They, too, were asked to respond by reproducing their previous answers. This tested the extent to which learning the correct answers distorted the subjects' memories of their own previous answers, thus measuring the same bias in recollection of previous estimates that was discussed above from the analyst's perspective.

The third group was given a different set of 25 questions they had not previously seen, but which were of similar difficulty so that results would be comparable with the other two groups. The correct answers were marked on the questionnaire, and the subjects were asked to respond to the questions as they would have responded had they not been told the answer. This tested their ability to recall accurately how much they had known before they learned the correct answer. The situation is comparable to that of intelligence consumers who are asked to evaluate how much they learned from a report, and who can do this only by trying to recollect the extent of their knowledge before they read the report.

The most significant results came from this third group of subjects. The group clearly overestimated what they had known originally and underestimated how much they learned from having been told the answer. For 19 of 25 items in one running of the experiment and 20 of 25 items in another running, this group assigned higher probabilities to the correct alternatives than it is reasonable to expect they would have assigned had they not already known the correct answers.

In summary, the experiment confirmed the results of the previous experiment showing that people exposed to an answer tend to remember having known more than they actually did. It also demonstrates that people have an even greater tendency to exaggerate the likelihood that they would have known the correct answer if they had not been informed of it. In other words, people tend to underestimate both how much they learn from new information and the extent to which new information permits them to make correct judgments with greater confidence. To the extent that intelligence consumers manifest these same biases, they will tend to underrate the value to them of intelligence reporting.

THE OVERSEER'S PERSPECTIVE

An overseer, as the term is used here, is one who investigates intelligence performance by conducting apostmortemexamination of a high-profile intelligence failure. Such investigations are carried out by Congress, the Intelligence Community staff, and CIA or DI management. For those outside the executive branch who do not regularly read the intelligence product, this sort of retrospective evaluation of known intelligence failures is a principal basis for judgments about the quality of intelligence analysis.

A fundamental question posed in anypostmorteminvestigation of intelligence failure is this: Given the information that was available at the time, should analysts have been able to foresee what was going to happen? Unbiased evaluation of intelligence performance depends upon the ability to provide an unbiased answer to this question.[152]

Unfortunately, once an event has occurred, it is impossible to erase from our mind the knowledge of that event and reconstruct what our thought processes would have been at an earlier point in time. In reconstructing the past, there is a tendency toward determinism, toward thinking that what occurred was inevitable under the circumstances and therefore predictable. In short, there is a tendency to believe analysts should have foreseen events that were, in fact, unforeseeable on the basis of the information available at the time.

The experiments reported in the following paragraphs tested the hypotheses that knowledge of an outcome increases the perceived inevitability of that outcome, and that people who are informed of the outcome are largely unaware that this information has changed their perceptions in this manner.

A series of sub-experiments used brief (150-word) summaries of several events for which four possible outcomes were identified. One of these events was the struggle between the British and the Gurkhas in India in 1814. The four possible outcomes for this event were 1) British victory, 2) Gurkha victory, 3) military stalemate with no peace settlement, and 4) military stalemate with a peace settlement. Five groups of 20 subjects each participated in each sub-experiment. One group received the 150-word description of the struggle between the British and the Gurkhas with no indication of the outcome. The other four groups received the identical description but with one sentence added to indicate the outcome of the struggle--a different outcome for each group.

The subjects in all five groups were asked to estimate the likelihood of each of the four possible outcomes and to evaluate the relevance to their judgment of each datum in the event description. Those subjects who were informed of an outcome were placed in the same position as an overseer of intelligence analysis preparing a postmortem analysis of an intelligence failure. This person tries to assess the probability of an outcome based only on the information available before the outcome was known. The results are shown in Figure 18.

The group not informed of any outcome judged the probability of Outcome 1 as 33.8 percent, while the group told that Outcome 1 was the actual outcome perceived the probability of this outcome as 57.2 percent. The estimated probability was clearly influenced by knowledge of the outcome. Similarly, the control group with no outcome knowledge estimated the probability of Outcome 2 as 21.3 percent, while those informed that Outcome 2 was the actual outcome perceived it as having a 38.4 percent probability.

Experimental Groups	Average Probabilities Assigned to Outcomes			
	1	2	3	4
Not Told Outcome	33.8	21.3	32.3	12.3
Told Outcome 1	57.2	14.3	15.3	13.4
Told Outcome 2	30.3	38.4	20.4	10.5
Told Outcome 3	25.7	17.0	48.4	9.9
Told Outcome 4	33.0	15.8	24.3	27.0

Figure 19

An average of all estimated outcomes in six sub-experiments (a total of 2,188 estimates by 547 subjects) indicates that the knowledge or belief that one of four possible outcomes has occurred approximately doubles the perceived probability of that outcome as judged with hindsight as compared with foresight.

The relevance that subjects attributed to any datum was also strongly influenced by which outcome, if any, they had been told was true. As Roberta Wohlstetter has written, "It is much easier after the fact to sort the relevant from the irrelevant signals. After the event, of course, a signal is always crystal clear. We can now see what disaster it was signaling since the disaster has occurred, but before the event it is obscure and pregnant with conflicting meanings."[153] The fact that outcome knowledge automatically restructures a person's judgments about the relevance of available data is probably one reason it is so difficult to reconstruct how our thought processes were or would have been without this outcome knowledge.

In several variations of this experiment, subjects were asked to respond as though they did not know the outcome, or as others would respond if they did not know the outcome. The results were little different, indicating that subjects were largely unaware of how knowledge of the outcome affected their own perceptions. The experiment showed that subjects were unable to empathize with how others would judge these situations. Estimates of how others would interpret the data without knowing the outcome were virtually the same as the test subjects' own retrospective interpretations.

These results indicate that overseers conducting postmortemevaluations of what analysts should have been able to foresee, given the available information, will tend to perceive the outcome of that situation as having been more predictable than was, in fact, the case. Because they are unable to reconstruct a state of mind that views the situation only with foresight, not hindsight, overseers will tend to be more critical of intelligence performance than is warranted.

DISCUSSION OF EXPERIMENTS

Experiments that demonstrated these biases and their resistance to corrective action were conducted as part of a research program in decision analysis funded by the Defense Advanced Research Projects Agency. Unfortunately, the experimental subjects were students, not members of the Intelligence Community. There is, nonetheless, reason to believe the results can be generalized to apply to the Intelligence Community. The experiments deal with basic human mental processes, and the results do seem consistent with personal experience in the Intelligence Community. In similar kinds of psychological tests, in which experts, including intelligence analysts, were used as test subjects, the experts showed the same pattern of responses as students.

My own imperfect effort to replicate one of these experiments using intelligence analysts also supports the validity of the previous findings. To test the assertion that intelligence analysts normally overestimate the accuracy of their past judgments, there are two necessary preconditions. First, analysts must make a series of estimates in quantitative terms--that is, they must say not just that a given occurrence is probable, but that there is, for example, a 75-percent chance of its occurrence. Second, it must be possible to make an unambiguous determination whether the estimated event did or did not occur. When these two preconditions are present, one can go back and check the analysts' recollections of their earlier estimates. Because CIA estimates are rarely stated in terms of quantitative probabilities, and because the occurrence of an estimated event within a specified time period often cannot be determined unambiguously, these preconditions are seldom met.

I did, however, identify several analysts who, on two widely differing subjects, had made quantitative estimates of the likelihood of events for which the subsequent outcome was clearly known. I went to these analysts and asked them to recall their earlier estimates. The conditions for this mini-experiment were far from ideal and the results were not clear-cut, but they did tend to support the conclusions drawn from the more extensive and systematic experiments described above.

All this leads to the conclusion that the three biases are found in Intelligence Community personnel as well as in the specific test subjects. In fact, one would expect the biases to be even greater in foreign affairs professionals whose careers and self-esteem depend upon the presumed accuracy of their judgments.

CAN WE OVERCOME THESE BIASES?

Analysts tend to blame biased evaluations of intelligence performance at best on ignorance and at worst on self-interest and lack of objectivity. Both these factors may also be at work, but the experiments suggest the nature of human mental processes is also a principal culprit. This is a more intractable cause than either ignorance or lack of objectivity.

The self-interest of the experimental subjects was not at stake, yet they showed the same kinds of bias with which analysts are familiar. Moreover, in these experimental situations the biases were highly resistant to efforts to overcome them. Subjects were instructed to make estimates as if they did not already know the answer, but they were unable to do so. One set of test subjects was briefed specifically on the bias, citing the results of previous experiments. This group was instructed to try to compensate for the bias, but it was unable to do so. Despite maximum information and the best of intentions, the bias persisted.

This intractability suggests the bias does indeed have its roots in the nature of our mental processes. Analysts who try to recall a previous estimate after learning the actual outcome of events, consumers who think about how much a report has added to their knowledge, and overseers who judge whether analysts should have been able to avoid an intelligence failure, all have one thing in common. They are engaged in a mental process involving hindsight. They are trying to erase the impact of knowledge, so as to remember, reconstruct, or imagine the uncertainties they had or would have had about a subject prior to receipt of more or less definitive information.

It appears, however, that the receipt of what is accepted as definitive or authoritative information causes an immediate but unconscious restructuring of a person's mental images to make them consistent with the new information. Once past perceptions have been restructured, it seems very difficult, if not impossible, to reconstruct accurately what one's thought processes were or would have been before this restructuring.

There is one procedure that may help to overcome these biases. It is to pose such questions as the following: Analysts should ask themselves, "If the opposite outcome had occurred, would I have been surprised?" Consumers should ask, "If this report had told me the opposite, would I have believed it?" And overseers should ask, "If the opposite outcome had occurred, would it have been predictable given the information that was available?" These questions may help one recall or reconstruct the uncertainty that existed prior to learning the content of a report or the outcome of a situation.

This method of overcoming the bias can be tested by readers of this chapter, especially those who believe it failed to tell them much they had not already known. If this chapter had reported that psychological experiments show no consistent pattern of analysts overestimating the accuracy of their estimates, or of consumers underestimating the value of our product, would you have believed it? (Answer: Probably not.) If it had reported that psychological experiments show these biases to be caused only by self-interest and lack of objectivity, would you have believed this? (Answer: Probably yes.) And would you have believed it if this chapter had reported these biases can be overcome by a conscientious effort at objective evaluation? (Answer: Probably yes.)

These questions may lead you, the reader, to recall the state of your knowledge or beliefs before reading this chapter. If so, the questions will highlight what you learned here--namely, that significant biases in the evaluation of intelligence estimates are attributable to the nature of human mental processes, not just to self-interest and lack of objectivity, and that they are, therefore, exceedingly difficult to overcome.

PART IV:
CONCLUSIONS

Chapter 14

IMPROVING INTELLIGENCE ANALYSIS

SUMMARY

This chapter offers a checklist for analysts--a summary of tips on how to navigate the minefield of problems identified in previous chapters. It also identifies steps that managers of intelligence analysis can take to help create an environment in which analytical excellence can flourish.

How can intelligence analysis be improved? That is the challenge. A variety of traditional approaches are used in pursuing this goal: collecting more and better information for analysts to work with, changing the management of the analytical process, increasing the number of analysts, providing language and area studies to improve analysts' substantive expertise, revising employee selection and retention criteria, improving report-writing skills, fine-tuning the relationship between intelligence analysts and intelligence consumers, and modifying the types of analytical products.

Any of these measures may play an important role, but analysis is, above all, a mental process. Traditionally, analysts at all levels devote little attention to improving how they think. To penetrate the heart and soul of the problem of improving analysis, it is necessary to better understand, influence, and guide the mental processes of analysts themselves.

CHECKLIST FOR ANALYSTS

This checklist for analysts summarizes guidelines for maneuvering through the minefields encountered while proceeding through the analytical process. Following the guidelines will help analysts protect themselves from avoidable error and improve their chances of making the right calls. The discussion is organized around six key steps in the analytical process: defining the problem, generating hypotheses, collecting information, evaluating hypotheses, selecting the most likely hypothesis, and the ongoing monitoring of new information.

Defining the Problem

Start out by making certain you are asking--or being asked--the right questions. Do not hesitate to go back up the chain of command with a suggestion for doing something a little different from what was asked for. The policymaker who originated the requirement may not have thought through his or her needs, or the requirement may be somewhat garbled as it passes down through several echelons of management. You may have a better understanding than the policymaker of what he or she needs, or should have, or what is possible to do. At the outset, also be sure your supervisor is aware of any tradeoff between quality of analysis and what you can accomplish within a specified time deadline.

Generating Hypotheses

Identify all the plausible hypotheses that need to be considered. Make a list of as many ideas as possible by consulting colleagues and outside experts. Do this in a brainstorming mode, suspending judgment for as long as possible until all the ideas are out on the table.

Then whittle the list down to a workable number of hypotheses for more detailed analysis. Frequently, one of these will be a deception hypothesis--that another country or group is engaging in denial and deception to influence US perceptions or actions.

At this stage, do not screen out reasonable hypotheses only because there is no evidence to support them. This applies in particular to the deception hypothesis. If another country is concealing its intent through denial and deception, you should probably not expect to see evidence of it without completing a very careful analysis of this possibility. The deception hypothesis and other plausible hypotheses for which there may be no immediate evidence should be carried forward to the next stage of analysis until they can be carefully considered and, if appropriate, rejected with good cause.

Collecting Information

Relying only on information that is automatically delivered to you will probably not solve all your analytical problems. To do the job right, it will probably be necessary to look elsewhere and dig for more information. Contact with the collectors, other Directorate of Operations personnel, or first-cut analysts often yields additional information. Also check academic specialists, foreign newspapers, and specialized journals.

Collect information to evaluate all the reasonable hypotheses, not just the one that seems most likely. Exploring alternative hypotheses that have not been seriously considered before often leads an analyst into unexpected and unfamiliar territory. For example, evaluating the possibility of deception requires evaluating another country's or group's motives, opportunities, and means for denial and deception. This, in turn, may require understanding the strengths and weaknesses of US human and technical collection capabilities.

It is important to suspend judgment while information is being assembled on each of the hypotheses. It is easy to form impressions about a hypothesis on the basis of very little information, but hard to change an impression once it has taken root. If you find yourself thinking you already know the answer, ask yourself what would cause you to change your mind; then look for that information.

Try to develop alternative hypotheses in order to determine if some alternative--when given a fair chance--might not be as compelling as your own preconceived view. Systematic development of an alternative hypothesis usually increases the perceived likelihood of that hypothesis. "A willingness to play with material from different angles and in the context of unpopular as well as popular hypotheses is an essential ingredient of a good detective, whether the end is the solution of a crime or an intelligence estimate."[154]

Evaluating Hypotheses

Do not be misled by the fact that so much evidence supports your preconceived idea of which is the most likely hypothesis. That same evidence may be consistent with several different hypotheses. Focus on developing arguments *against* each hypothesis rather than trying to confirm hypotheses. In other words, pay particular attention to evidence or assumptions that suggest one or more hypotheses are *less* likely than the others.

Recognize that your conclusions may be driven by assumptions that determine how you interpret the evidence rather than by the evidence itself. Especially critical are assumptions about what is in another country's national interest and how things are usually done in that country. Assumptions are fine as long as they are made explicit in your analysis and you analyze the sensitivity of your conclusions to those assumptions. Ask yourself, would different assumptions lead to a different interpretation of the evidence and different conclusions?

Consider using the matrix format discussed in Chapter 8, "Analysis of Competing Hypotheses," to keep track of the evidence and how it relates to the various hypotheses.

Guard against the various cognitive biases. Especially dangerous are those biases that occur when you lack sufficient understanding of how a situation appears from another country's point of view. Do not fill gaps in your knowledge by assuming that the other side is likely to act in a certain way because that is how the US Government would act, or other Americans would act, under similar circumstances.

Recognize that the US perception of another country's national interest and decisionmaking processes often differs from how that country perceives its own interests and how decisions are actually made in that country. In 1989-90, for example, many analysts of Middle Eastern affairs clearly assumed that Iraq would demobilize part of its armed forces after the lengthy Iran-Iraq war so as to help rehabilitate the Iraqi economy. They also believed Baghdad would see that attacking a neighboring Arab country would not be in Iraq's best interest. We now know they were wrong.

When making a judgment about what another country is likely to do, invest whatever time and effort are needed to consult with whichever experts have the best understanding of what that country's government is actually thinking and how the decision is likely to be made.

Do not assume that every foreign government action is based on a rational decision in pursuit of identified goals. Recognize that government actions are sometimes best explained as a product of bargaining among semi-independent bureaucratic entities, following standard operating procedures under inappropriate circumstances, unintended consequences, failure to follow orders, confusion, accident, or coincidence.

Selecting the most Likely Hypothesis

Proceed by trying to reject hypotheses rather than confirm them. The most likely hypothesis is usually the one with the least evidence against it, not the one with the most evidence for it.

In presenting your conclusions, note all the reasonable hypotheses that were considered. Cite the arguments and evidence supporting your judgment, but also justify briefly why other alternatives were rejected or considered less likely. To avoid ambiguity, insert an odds ratio or probability range in parentheses after expressions of uncertainty in key judgments.

Ongoing Monitoring

In a rapidly changing, probabilistic world, analytical conclusions are always tentative. The situation may change, or it may remain unchanged while you receive new information that alters your understanding of it. Specify things to look for that, if observed, would suggest a significant change in the probabilities.

Pay particular attention to any feeling of surprise when new information does not fit your prior understanding. Consider whether this surprising information is consistent with an alternative hypothesis. A surprise or two, however small, may be the first clue that your understanding of what is happening requires some adjustment, is at best incomplete, or may be quite wrong.

MANAGEMENT OF ANALYSIS

The cognitive problems described in this book have implications for the management as well as the conduct of intelligence analysis. This concluding section looks at what managers of intelligence analysis can do to help create an organizational environment in which analytical excellence flourishes. These measures fall into four general categories: research, training, exposure to alternative mind-sets, and guiding analytical products.

Support for Research

Management should support research to gain a better understanding of the cognitive processes involved in making intelligence judgments. There is a need for better understanding of the thinking skills involved in intelligence analysis, how to test job applicants for these skills, and how to train analysts to improve these skills. Analysts also need a fuller understanding of how cognitive limitations affect intelligence analysis and how to minimize their impact. They need simple tools and techniques to help protect themselves from avoidable error. There is so much research to be done that it is difficult to know where to start.

Scholars selected for tours of duty in the Intelligence Community should include cognitive psychologists or other scholars of various backgrounds who are interested in studying the thinking processes of intelligence analysts. There should also be post-doctoral fellowships for promising scholars who could be encouraged to make a career of research in this field. Over time, this would contribute to building a better base of knowledge about how analysts do and/or should make analytical judgments and what tools or techniques can help them.

Management should also support research on the mind-sets and implicit mental models of intelligence analysts. Because these mind-sets or models serve as a "screen" or "lens" through which analysts perceive foreign developments, research to determine the nature of this "lens" may contribute as much to accurate judgments as does research focused more directly on the foreign areas themselves.[155]

Training

Most training of intelligence analysts is focused on organizational procedures, writing style, and methodological techniques. Analysts who write clearly are assumed to be thinking clearly. Yet it is quite possible to follow a faulty analytical process and write a clear and persuasive argument in support of an erroneous judgment.

More training time should be devoted to the thinking and reasoning processes involved in making intelligence judgments, and to the tools of the trade that are available to alleviate or compensate for the known cognitive problems encountered in analysis. This book is intended to support such training.

Training will be more effective if supplemented with ongoing advice and assistance. An experienced coach who can monitor and guide ongoing performance is a valuable supplement to classroom instruction in many fields, probably including intelligence analysis. This is supposed to be the job of the branch chief or senior analyst, but these officers are often too busy responding to other pressing demands on their time.

It would be worthwhile to consider how an analytical coaching staff might be formed to mentor new analysts or consult with analysts working particularly difficult issues. One possible model is the SCORE organization that exists in many communities. SCORE stands for Senior Corps of Retired Executives. It is a national organization of retired executives who volunteer their time to counsel young entrepreneurs starting their own businesses. It should be possible to form a small group of retired analysts who possess the skills and values that should be imparted to new analysts, and who would be willing to volunteer (or be hired) to come in several days a week to counsel junior analysts.

New analysts could be required to read a specified set of books or articles relating to analysis, and to attend a half-day meeting once a month to discuss the reading and other experiences related to their development as analysts. A comparable voluntary program could be conducted for experienced analysts. This would help make analysts more conscious of the procedures they use in doing analysis. In addition to their educational value, the required readings and discussion would give analysts a common experience and vocabulary for communicating with each other, and with management, about the problems of doing analysis.

My suggestions for writings that would qualify for a mandatory reading program include: Robert Jervis' *Perception and Misperception in International Politics* (Princeton University Press, 1977); Graham Allison's *Essence of Decision: Explaining the Cuban Missile Crisis* (Little, Brown, 1971); Ernest May's *"Lessons" of the Past: The Use and Misuse of History in American Foreign Policy* (Oxford University Press, 1973); Ephraim Kam's, *Surprise Attack* (Harvard University Press, 1988); Richard Betts' "Analysis, War and Decision: Why Intelligence Failures Are Inevitable," *World Politics,* Vol. 31, No. 1 (October 1978); Thomas Kuhn's *The Structure of Scientific Revolutions* (University of Chicago Press, 1970); and Robin Hogarth's *Judgement and Choice* (John Wiley, 1980). Although these were all written many years ago, they are classics of permanent value. Current analysts will doubtless have other works to recommend. CIA and Intelligence Community postmortem analyses of intelligence failure should also be part of the reading program.

To facilitate institutional memory and learning, thorough postmortem analyses should be conducted on all significant intelligence failures. Analytical (as distinct from collection) successes should also be studied. These analyses should be collated and maintained in a central location, available for review to identify the common characteristics of analytical failure and success. A meta-analysis of the causes and consequences of analytical success and failure should be widely distributed and used in training programs to heighten awareness of analytical problems.

To encourage learning from experience, even in the absence of a high-profile failure, management should require more frequent and systematic retrospective evaluation of analytical performance. One ought not generalize from any single instance of a correct or incorrect judgment, but a series of related judgments that are, or are not, borne out by subsequent events can reveal the accuracy or inaccuracy of the analyst's mental model. Obtaining systematic feedback on the accuracy of past judgments is frequently difficult or impossible, especially in the political intelligence field. Political judgments are normally couched in imprecise terms and are generally conditional upon other developments. Even in retrospect, there are no objective criteria for evaluating the accuracy of most political intelligence judgments as they are presently written.

In the economic and military fields, however, where estimates are frequently concerned with numerical quantities, systematic feedback on analytical performance is feasible. Retrospective evaluation should be standard procedure in those fields in which estimates are routinely updated at periodic intervals. The goal of learning from retrospective evaluation is achieved, however, only if it is accomplished as part of an objective search for improved understanding, not to identify scapegoats or assess blame. This requirement suggests that retrospective evaluation should be done routinely within the organizational unit that prepared the report, even at the cost of some loss of objectivity.

Exposure to Alternative Mind-sets

The realities of bureaucratic life produce strong pressures for conformity. Management needs to make conscious efforts to ensure that well-reasoned competing views have the opportunity to surface within the Intelligence Community. Analysts need to enjoy a sense of security, so that partially developed new ideas may be expressed and bounced off others as sounding boards with minimal fear of criticism for deviating from established orthodoxy.

Much of this book has dealt with ways of helping analysts remain more open to alternative views. Management can help by promoting the kinds of activities that confront analysts with alternative perspectives--consultation with outside experts, analytical debates, competitive analysis, devil's advocates, gaming, and interdisciplinary brainstorming.

Consultation with outside experts is especially important as a means of avoiding what Adm. David Jeremiah called the "everybody-thinks-like-us mindset" when making significant judgments that depend upon knowledge of a foreign culture. Intelligence analysts have often spent less time living in and absorbing the culture of the countries they are working on than outside experts on those countries. If analysts fail to understand the foreign culture, they will not see issues as the foreign government sees them. Instead, they may be inclined to mirror-image--that is, to assume that the other country's leaders think like we do. The analyst assumes that the other country will do what we would do if we were in their shoes.

Mirror-imaging is a common source of analytical error, and one that reportedly played a role in the Intelligence Community failure to warn of imminent Indian nuclear weapons testing in 1998. After leading a US Government team that analyzed this episode, Adm. Jeremiah recommended more systematic use of outside expertise whenever there is a major transition that may lead to policy changes, such as the Hindu nationalists' 1998 election victory and ascension to power in India.[156]

Pre-publication review of analytical reports offers another opportunity to bring alternative perspectives to bear on an issue. Review procedures should explicitly question the mental model employed by the analyst in searching for and examining evidence. What assumptions has the analyst made that are not discussed in the draft itself, but that underlie the principal judgments? What alternative hypotheses have been considered but rejected, and for what reason? What could cause the analyst to change his or her mind?

Ideally, the review process should include analysts from other areas who are not specialists in the subject matter of the report. Analysts within the same branch or division often share a similar mind-set. Past experience with review by analysts from other divisions or offices indicates that critical thinkers whose expertise is in other areas make a significant contribution. They often see things or ask questions that the author has not seen or asked. Because they are not so absorbed in the substance, they are better able to identify the assumptions and assess the argumentation, internal consistency, logic, and relationship of the evidence to the conclusion. The reviewers also profit from the experience by learning standards for good analysis that are independent of the subject matter of the analysis.

Guiding Analytical Products

On key issues, management should reject most single-outcome analysis--that is, the single-minded focus on what the analyst believes is probably happening or most likely will happen. When we cannot afford to get it wrong, or when deception is a serious possibility, management should consider mandating a systematic analytical process such as the one described in Chapter 8, "Analysis of Competing Hypotheses." Analysts should be required to identify alternatives that were considered, justify why the alternatives are deemed less likely, and clearly express the degree of likelihood that events may not turn out as expected.

Even if the analyst firmly believes the odds are, say, three-to-one against something happening, that leaves a 25-percent chance that it will occur. Making this explicit helps to better define the problem for the policymaker. Does that 25-percent chance merit some form of contingency planning?

If the less likely hypothesis happens to be, for example, that a new Indian Government will actually follow through on its election campaign promise to conduct nuclear weapons testing, as recently occurred, even a 25-percent chance might be sufficient to put technical collection systems on increased alert.

Verbal expressions of uncertainty--such as possible, probable, unlikely, may, and could--have long been recognized as sources of ambiguity and misunderstanding. By themselves, most verbal expressions of uncertainty are empty shells. The reader or listener fills them with meaning through the context in which they are used and what is already in the reader's or listener's mind about that subject. An intelligence consumer's interpretation of imprecise probability judgments will always be biased in favor of consistency with what the reader already believes. That means the intelligence reports will be undervalued and have little impact on the consumer's judgment. This ambiguity can be especially troubling when dealing with low-probability, high-impact dangers against which policymakers may wish to make contingency plans.

Managers of intelligence analysis need to convey to analysts that it is okay to be uncertain, as long as they clearly inform readers of the degree of uncertainty, sources of uncertainty, and what milestones to watch for that might clarify the situation. Inserting odds ratios or numerical probability ranges in parentheses to clarify key points of an analysis should be standard practice.

The likelihood of future surprises can be reduced if management assigns more resources to monitoring and analyzing seemingly low-probability events that will have a significant impact on US policy if they do occur. Analysts are often reluctant, on their own initiative, to devote time to studying things they do not believe will happen. This usually does not further an analyst's career, although it can ruin a career when the unexpected does happen. Given the day-to-day pressures of current events, it is necessary for managers and analysts to clearly identify which unlikely but high-impact events need to be analyzed and to allocate the resources to cover them.

One guideline for identifying unlikely events that merit the specific allocation of resources is to ask the following question: Are the chances of this happening, however small, sufficient that if policymakers fully understood the risks, they might want to make contingency plans or take some form of preventive or preemptive action? If the answer is yes, resources should be committed to analyze even what appears to be an unlikely outcome.

Managers of intelligence should support analyses that periodically re-examine key problems from the ground up in order to avoid the pitfalls of the incremental approach. Receipt of information in small increments over time facilitates assimilation of this information to the analyst's existing views. No one item of information may be sufficient to prompt the analyst to change a previous view. The cumulative message inherent in many pieces of information may be significant but is attenuated when this information is not examined as a whole.

Finally, management should educate consumers concerning the limitations as well as the capabilities of intelligence analysis and should define a set of realistic expectations as a standard against which to judge analytical performance.

THE BOTTOM LINE

Analysis can be improved! None of the measures discussed in this book will guarantee that accurate conclusions will be drawn from the incomplete and ambiguous information that intelligence analysts typically work with. Occasional intelligence failures must be expected. Collectively, however, the measures discussed here can certainly improve the odds in the analysts' favor.

REFERENCES

[1] Jack Davis served with the Directorate of Intelligence (DI), the National Intelligence Council, and the Office of Training during his CIA career. He is now an independent contractor who specializes in developing and teaching analytic tradecraft. Among his publications is *Uncertainty, Surprise, and Warning* (1996).

[2] See, in particular, the editor's unclassified introductory essay and "Tribute" by Harold P. Ford in Donald P. Steury, *Sherman Kent and the Board of National Estimates: Collected Essays* (CIA, Center for the Study of Intelligence, 1994). Hereinafter cited as Steury, *Kent.*

[3] Sherman Kent, *Writing History*, second edition (1967). The first edition was published in 1941, when Kent was an assistant professor of history at Yale. In the first chapter, "Why History," he presented ideas and recommendations that he later adapted for intelligence analysis.

[4] Kent, "Estimates and Influence" (1968), in Steury, *Kent.*

[5] Casey, very early in his tenure as DCI (1981-1987), opined to me that the trouble with Agency analysts is that they went from sitting on their rear ends at universities to sitting on their rear ends at CIA, without seeing the real world.

[6] "The Gates Hearings: Politicization and Soviet Analysis at CIA", *Studies in Intelligence* (Spring 1994). "Communication to the Editor: The Gates Hearings: A Biased Account," *Studies in Intelligence* (Fall 1994).

[7] DCI Casey requested that the Agency's training office provide this seminar so that, at the least, analysts could learn from their own mistakes. DDI Gates carefully reviewed the statement of goals for the seminar, the outline of course units, and the required reading list.

[8]   Unclassified paper published in 1994 by the Working Group on Intelligence Reform, which had been created in 1992 by the Consortium for the Study of Intelligence, Washington, DC.

[9]   Discussion between MacEachin and the author of this Introduction, 1994.

[10]   Letter to the author of this Introduction, 1998.

[11]   James L. Adams, *Conceptual Blockbusting: A Guide to Better Ideas* (New York: W.W. Norton, second edition, 1980), p. 3.

[12]   Herbert Simon, *Models of Man*, 1957.

[13]   James G. March., "Bounded Rationality, Ambiguity, and the Engineering of Choice," in David E. Bell, Howard Raiffa, and Amos Tversky, eds., *Decision Making: Descriptive, Normative, and Prescriptive Interactions* (Cambridge University Press, 1988).

[14]   Among the early scholars who wrote on this subject were Joseph De Rivera, *The Psychological Dimension of Foreign Policy* (Columbus, OH: Merrill, 1968), Alexander George and Richard Smoke, *Deterrence in American Foreign Policy* (New York: Columbia University Press, 1974), and Robert Jervis, *Perception and Misperception in International Politics* (Princeton, NJ: Princeton University Press, 1976).

[15]   Christopher Brady, "Intelligence Failures: Plus Ca Change. . ." Intelligence and National Security, Vol. 8, No. 4 (October 1993). N. Cigar, "Iraq's Strategic Mindset and the Gulf War: Blueprint for Defeat," *The Journal of Strategic Studies*, Vol. 15, No. 1 (March 1992). J. J. Wirtz, *The Tet Offensive: Intelligence Failure in War* (New York, 1991). Ephraim Kam, *Surprise Attack* (Harvard University Press, 1988). Richard Betts, *Surprise Attack: Lessons for Defense Planning* (Brookings, 1982). Abraham Ben-Zvi, "The Study of Surprise Attacks," *British Journal of International Studies*, Vol. 5 (1979). *Iran: Evaluation of Intelligence Performance Prior to November 1978* (Staff Report, Subcommittee on Evaluation, Permanent Select Committee on Intelligence, US House of Representatives, January 1979). Richard Betts, "Analysis, War and Decision: Why Intelligence Failures Are Inevitable," *World Politics*, Vol. 31, No. 1 (October 1978). Richard W. Shryock, "The Intelligence Community Post-Mortem Program, 1973-1975," *Studies in Intelligence*, Vol. 21, No. 1 (Fall 1977). Avi Schlaim, "Failures in National Intelligence Estimates: The Case of the Yom Kippur War," *World Politics*, Vol. 28 (April 1976). Michael Handel, *Perception, Deception, and Surprise: The Case of the Yom Kippur War*

(Jerusalem: Leonard Davis Institute of International Relations, Jerusalem Paper No. 19, 1976). Klaus Knorr, "Failures in National Intelligence Estimates: The Case of the Cuban Missiles," *World Politics*, Vol. 16 (1964).

[16] This wording is from a discussion with veteran CIA analyst, author, and teacher Jack Davis.

[17] Graham Allison's work on the Cuban missile crisis (*Essence of Decision*, Little, Brown & Co., 1971) is an example of what I have in mind. Allison identified three alternative assumptions about how governments work--a rational actor model, an organizational process model, and a bureaucratic politics model. He then showed how an analyst's implicit assumptions about the most appropriate model for analyzing a foreign government's behavior can cause him or her to focus on different evidence and arrive at different conclusions. Another example is my own analysis of five alternative paths for making counterintelligence judgments in the controversial case of KGB defector Yuriy Nosenko: Richards J. Heuer, Jr., "Nosenko: Five Paths to Judgment," *Studies in Intelligence*, Vol. 31, No. 3 (Fall 1987), originally classified Secret but declassified and published in H. Bradford Westerfield, ed., *Inside CIA's Private World: DeclassifiedArticles from the Agency's Internal Journal 1955-1992* (New Haven: Yale University Press, 1995).

[18] An earlier version of this article was published as part of "Cognitive Factors in Deception and Counterdeception," in Donald C. Daniel and Katherine L. Herbig, eds., *Strategic Military Deception* (Pergamon Press, 1982).

[19] The article is written twice in each of the three phrases. This is commonly overlooked because perception is influenced by our expectations about how these familiar phrases are normally written.

[20] Jerome S. Bruner and Leo Postman, "On the Perception of Incongruity: A Paradigm," in Jerome S. Bruner and David Kraut, eds., *Perception and Personality: A Symposium* (New York: Greenwood Press, 1968).

[21] For discussion of the ambiguous evidence concerning the impact of desires and fears on judgment, see Robert Jervis, *Perception and Misperception in International Politics* (Princeton, NJ: Princeton University Press, 1976), Chapter 10.

[22] Richard Betts, "Analysis, War and Decision: Why Intelligence Failures are Inevitable", *World Politics*, Vol. XXXI (October 1978), p. 84.

[23] Drawings devised by Gerald Fisher in 1967.

[24] Jervis, p. 195.

[25] This picture was originally published in *Puck* magazine in 1915 as a cartoon entitled "My Wife and My Mother-in-Law."

[26] The old woman's nose, mouth, and eye are, respectively, the young woman's chin, necklace, and ear. The old woman is seen in profile looking left. The young woman is also looking left, but we see her mainly from behind so most facial features are not visible. Her eyelash, nose, and the curve of her cheek may be seen just above the old woman's nose.

[27] Jerome S. Bruner and Mary C. Potter, "Interference in Visual Recognition," *Science*, Vol. 144 (1964), pp. 424-25.

[28] *The Performance of the Intelligence Community Before the Arab-Israeli War of October 1973: A Preliminary Post-Mortem Report,* December 1973. The one-paragraph excerpt from this post-mortem, as quoted in the text above, has been approved for public release, as was the title of the post-mortem, although that document as a whole remains classified.

[29] Memory researchers do not employ uniform terminology. Sensory information storage is also known as sensory register, sensory store, and eidetic and echoic memory. Short- and long-term memory are also referred to as primary and secondary memory. A variety of other terms are in use as well. I have adopted the terminology used by Peter H. Lindsay and Donald A. Norman in their text on *Human Information Processing* (New York: Academic Press, 1977). This entire chapter draws heavily from Chapters 8 through 11 of the Lindsay and Norman book.

[30] George Johnson, *In the Palaces of Memory: How We Build the Worlds Inside Our Heads.* Vintage Books, 1992, p. xi.

[31] A. D. deGroot, *Thought and Choice in Chess* (The Hague: Mouton, 1965) cited by Herbert A. Simon, "How Big Is a Chunk?" *Science*, Vol. 183 (1974), p. 487.

[32] This discussion draws on Francis S. Bellezza, "Mnemonic Devices: Classification, Characteristics, and Criteria" (Athens, Ohio: Ohio University, pre-publication manuscript, January 1980).

[33] Arthur S. Elstein, Lee S. Shulman & Sarah A. Sprafka, *Medical Problem Solving: An Analysis of Clinical Reasoning* (Cambridge, MA: Harvard University Press, 1978), p. 276.

[34] George A. Miller, "The Magical Number Seven--Plus or Minus Two: Some Limits on our Capacity for Processing Information." *The Psychological Review*, Vol. 63, No. 2 (March 1956).

[35] Robert Tucker, "Communist Revolutions, National Cultures, and the Divided Nations," *Studies in Comparative Communism* (Autumn 1974), 235-245.

[36] An earlier version of this chapter was published as an unclassified article in *Studies in Intelligence* in 1981, under the title "Strategies for Analytical Judgment."

[37] Webster's *New International Dictionary*, unabridged, 1954.

[38] Even in retrospect these two propositions still seem valid, which is why some aspects of the Shah's fall remain incredible. There are, in principle, three possible reasons why these seemingly valid theoretical assumptions failed to generate an accurate estimate on Iran: (1) One or more of the initial conditions posited by the theory did not in fact apply--for example, the Shah was not really an authoritarian ruler. (2) The theory is only partially valid, in that there are certain circumstances under which it does and does not apply. These limiting conditions need to be specified. (3) The theory is basically valid, but one cannot expect 100-percent accuracy from social science theories. Social science, as distinct from natural science, deals with a probabilistic environment. One cannot foresee all the circumstances that might cause an exception to the general rules, so the best that can be expected is that the given conditions will lead to the specified outcome most of the time.

[39] Robert Jervis, "Hypotheses on Misperception," *World Politics* 20 (April 1968), p. 471.

[40] Ernest May, `Lessons' of the Past: The Use and Misuse of History in American Foreign Policy (New York: Oxford University Press, 1973).

[41] Ibid., p. xi.

[42] Arthur S. Elstein, Lee S. Shulman, and Sarah A. Sprafka, *Medical Problem Solving: An Analysis of Clinical Reasoning* (Cambridge, MA: Harvard University Press, 1978), p. 270.

[43] Ibid., p. 281. For more extensive discussion of the value of additional information, see Chapter 5, "Do You Really Need More Information?"

[44] Alexander George, Presidential Decisionmaking in Foreign Policy: The Effective Use of Information and Advice (Boulder, CO: Westview Press, 1980), Chapter 2.

[45]   The concept of "satisficing," of seeking a satisfactory rather than an optimal solution, was developed by Herbert A. Simon and is widely used in the literature on decision analysis.

[46]   Charles Gettys et al., *Hypothesis Generation: A Final Report on Three Years of Research*. Technical Report 15-10-80. University of Oklahoma, Decision Processes Laboratory, 1980.

[47]   P. C. Wason, "On the Failure to Eliminate Hypotheses in a Conceptual Task," *The Quarterly Journal of Experimental Psychology*, Vol. XII, Part 3 (1960).

[48]   Wason, ibid.

[49]   Harold M. Weiss and Patrick A. Knight, "The Utility of Humility: Self-Esteem, Information Search, and Problem-Solving Efficiency," *Organizational Behavior and Human Performance*, Vol. 25, No. 2 (April 1980), 216-223.

[50]   Alexander George, Propaganda Analysis: A Study of Inferences Made From Nazi Propaganda in World War II (Evanston, IL: Row, Peterson, 1959); Patrick Beesly, Very Special Intelligence: The Story of the Admiralty's Operational Intelligence Center 1939-1945 (London: Hamish Hamilton, 1977); and R. V. Jones, Wizard War: British Scientific Intelligence 1939-1945 (New York: Coward, McCann & Geoghegan, 1978).

[51]   Frank J. Stech, Political and Military Intention Estimation: A Taxonometric Analysis, Final Report for Office of Naval Research (Bethesda, MD: MATHTECH, Inc., November 1979), p. 283.

[52]   This is an edited version of an article that appeared in *Studies in Intelligence*, Vol. 23, No. 1 (Spring 1979). That *Studies in Intelligence* article was later reprinted in H. Bradford Westerfield, ed., *Inside CIA's Private World: Declassified Articles from the Agency's Internal Journal*, 1955-1992 (New Haven: Yale University Press, 1995). A slightly different version was published in *The Bureaucrat*, Vol. 8, 1979, under the title "Improving Intelligence Analysis: Some Insights on Data, Concepts, and Management in the Intelligence Community." For this book, portions of the original article dealing with improving intelligence analysis have been moved to Chapter 14 on "Improving Intelligence Analysis."

[53]   Paul Slovic, "Behavioral Problems of Adhering to a Decision Policy," unpublished manuscript, 1973.

[54]   For a list of references, see Lewis R. Goldberg, "Simple Models or Simple Processes? Some Research on Clinical Judgments," *American Psychologist*, 23 (1968), pp. 261-265.

[55] Stuart Oskamp, "Overconfidence in Case-Study Judgments," *Journal of Consulting Psychology*, 29 (1965), pp. 261-265.

[56] Arthur S. Elstein *et al., Medical Problem Solving: An Analysis of Clinical Reasoning* (Cambridge, MA and London: Harvard University Press, 1978), pp. 270 and 295.

[57] Paul Slovic, Dan Fleissner, and W. Scott Bauman, "Analyzing the Use of Information in Investment Decision Making: A Methodological Proposal," *The Journal of Business*, 45 (1972), pp. 283-301.

[58] For a discussion of the methodology, see Slovic, Fleissner, and Bauman, op. cit.

[59] For a list of references, see Paul Slovic and Sarah Lichtenstein, "Comparison of Bayesian and Regression Approaches to the Study of Information Processing in Judgment," *Organizational Behavior and Human Performance*, 6 (1971), p. 684.

[60] David A. Summers, J. Dale Taliaferro, and Donna J. Fletcher, "Subjective vs. Objective Description of Judgment Policy," *Psychonomic Science*, 18 (1970) pp. 249-250.

[61] R. N. Shepard, "On Subjectively Optimum Selection Among Multiattribute Alternatives," in M. W. Shelly, II and G. L. Bryan, eds., *Human Judgments and Optimality* (New York: Wiley, 1964), p. 166.

[62] This refers, of course, to subconscious processes. No analyst will consciously distort information that does not fit his or her preconceived beliefs. Important aspects of the perception and processing of new information occur prior to and independently of any conscious direction, and the tendencies described here are largely the result of these subconscious or preconscious processes.

[63] A similar point has been made in rebutting the belief in the accumulated wisdom of the classroom teacher. "It is actually very difficult for teachers to profit from experience. They almost never learn about their long-term successes or failures, and their short-term effects are not easily traced to the practices from which they presumably arose." B. F. Skinner, *The Technology of Teaching* (New York: Appleton-Century Crofts, 1968), pp. 112-113.

[64] Christopher Brady, "Intelligence Failures: Plus Ca Change. . ." *Intelligence and National Security*, Vol. 8, No. 4 (October 1993). N. Cigar, "Iraq's Strategic Mindset and the Gulf War: Blueprint for Defeat," *The Journal of Strategic Studies*, Vol. 15, No. 1 (March 1992). J. J. Wirtz, *The Tet Offensive: Intelligence Failure in War* (New York, 1991). Ephraim Kam, *Surprise Attack* (Harvard University Press, 1988). Richard Betts, *Surprise Attack: Lessons for*

Defense Planning (Brookings, 1982). Abraham Ben-Zvi, "The Study of Surprise Attacks," *British Journal of International Studies*, Vol. 5 (1979). *Iran: Evaluation of Intelligence Performance Prior to November 1978* (Staff Report, Subcommittee on Evaluation, Permanent Select Committee on Intelligence, US House of Representatives, January 1979). Richard Betts, "Analysis, War and Decision: Why Intelligence Failures Are Inevitable," *World Politics*, Vol. 31, No. 1 (October 1978). Richard W. Shryock, "The Intelligence Community Post-Mortem Program, 1973-1975," *Studies in Intelligence*, Vol. 21, No. 1 (Fall 1977). Avi Schlaim, "Failures in National Intelligence Estimates: The Case of the Yom Kippur War," *World Politics*, Vol. 28 (April 1976). Michael Handel, *Perception, Deception, and Surprise: The Case of the Yom Kippur War* (Jerusalem: Leonard Davis Institute of International Relations, Jerusalem Paper No. 19, 1976). Klaus Knorr, "Failures in National Intelligence Estimates: The Case of the Cuban Missiles," World Politics, Vol. 16 (1964).

[65] Roberta Wohlstetter, *Pearl Harbor: Warning and Decision* (Stanford University Press, 1962). Roberta Wohlstetter, "Cuba and Pearl Harbor: Hindsight and Foresight," *Foreign Affairs*, Vol. 43, No. 4 (July 1965).

[66] S. A. Mednick, "The Associative Basis of the Creative Process," *Psychological Review*, Vol. 69 (1962), p. 221.

[67] Jerry E. Bishop, "Stroke Patients Yield Clues to Brain's Ability to Create Language," *Wall Street Journal*, Oct. 12, 1993, p.A1.

[68] The puzzle is from James L. Adams, *Conceptual Blockbusting: A Guide to Better Ideas*. Second Edition (New York: W. W. Norton, 1980), p. 23.

[69] Jim Wolf, "CIA Inquest Finds US Missed Indian `Mindset'," UPI wire service, June 3, 1998.

[70] Discussion with Robert Jaster, former National Intelligence Officer for Southern Africa.

[71] Jon Fallesen, Rex Michel, James Lussier, and Julia Pounds, "Practical Thinking: Innovation in Battle Command Instruction" *(Technical Report 1037, US Army Research Institute for the Behavioral and Social Sciences*, January 1996).

[72] For an interesting discussion of the strengths and potential weaknesses of the "devil's advocate" approach, see Robert Jervis, *Perception and Misperception in International Politics* (Princeton, NJ: Princeton University Press, 1976), pp. 415-418.

[73] Daniel J. Isenberg, "How Senior Managers Think," in David Bell, Howard Raiffa, and Amos Tversky, *Decision Making: Descriptive, Normative, and Prescriptive Interactions* (Cambridge University Press, 1988), p. 535.

[74] Abraham Ben Zvi, "Hindsight and Foresight: A Conceptual Framework for the Analysis of Surprise Attacks," *World Politics*, April 1976.

[75] Transcript of Admiral David Jeremiah's news conference on the Intelligence Community's performance concerning the Indian nuclear test, fourth and fifth paragraphs and first Q and A, 2 June 1998.

[76] Frank M. Andrews, "Social and Psychological Factors Which Influence the Creative Process," in Irving A. Taylor and Jacob W. Getzels, eds., *Perspectives in Creativity* (Chicago, Aldine Publishing, 1975).

[77] Ibid., p. 122.

[78] Robin Hogarth, *Judgment and Choice* (New York: Wiley, 1980), p. 117.

[79] George A. Miller, "The Magical Number Seven, Plus or Minus Two: Some Limits on our Capacity for Processing Information." *The Psychological Review*, Vol. 63, No. 2 (March 1956).

[80] Webster's Ninth New Collegiate Dictionary, 1988.

[81] Howard Raiffa, *Decision Analysis* (Reading, MA: Addison-Wesley, 1968).

[82] J. Bigelow, ed., *The Complete Works of Benjamin Franklin* (New York: Putnam, 1887), p. 522.

[83] Alex Osborn, *Applied Imagination*, Revised Edition (New York: Scribner's, 1979), p. 202.

[84] The analysis of competing hypotheses procedure was developed by the author for use by intelligence analysts dealing with a set of particularly difficult problems.

[85] Charles Gettys et al., *Hypothesis Generation: A Final Report on Three Years of Research*, Technical Report 15-10-80 (University of Oklahoma, Decision Processes Laboratory, 1980).

[86] Transcript of Adm. Jeremiah's news conference, last sentence of third paragraph, 2 June 1998.

[87] M. Rogers, ed., *Contradictory Quotations* (England: Longman Group, Ltd., 1983).

[88] Much of this research was stimulated by the seminal work of Amos Tversky and Daniel Kahneman, "Judgment under Uncertainty: Heuristics and Biases," *Science*, 27 September 1974, Vol. 185, pp.

1124-1131. It has been summarized by Robin Hogarth, *Judgement and Choice* (New York: John Wiley & Sons, 1980), Richard Nisbett and Lee Ross, *Human Inference: Strategies and Shortcomings of Human Judgment* (Englewood Cliffs, NJ: Prentice-Hall, 1980), and Robyn Dawes, *Rational Choice in an Uncertain World* (New York: Harcourt Brace Jovanovich College Publishers, 1988). The Hogarth book contains an excellent bibliography of research in this field, organized by subject.

[89] Tversky and Kahneman, ibid.

[90] An earlier version of this chapter was published as an unclassified article in *Studies in Intelligence* in summer 1981, under the same title.

[91] Most of the ideas and examples in this section are from Richard Nisbett and Lee Ross, *Human Inference: Strategies and Shortcomings of Social Judgment* (Englewood Cliffs, NJ: Prentice-Hall, 1980), Chapter 3.

[92] A. Paivio, *Imagery and Verbal Processes* (New York: Holt, Rinehart & Winston, 1971).

[93] Nisbett and Ross, p. 56.

[94] Ibid.

[95] Nisbett and Ross, p. 57.

[96] Baruch Fischhoff, Paul Slovic, and Sarah Lichtenstein, *Fault Trees: Sensitivity of Estimated Failure Probabilities to Problem Representation*, Technical Report PTR- 1 042-77-8 (Eugene, OR: Decision Research, 1977).

[97] Amos Tversky and Daniel Kahneman, "Judgment under Uncertainty: Heuristics and Biases," *Science*, Vol. 185 (27 September 1974), 1126.

[98] Tversky and Kahneman (1974), p. 1125-1126.

[99] See Charles F. Gettys, Clinton W. Kelly III, and Cameron Peterson, "The Best Guess Hypothesis in Multistage Inference," *Organizational Behavior and Human Performance, 10*, 3 (1973), 365-373; and David A. Schum and Wesley M. DuCharme, "Comments on the Relationship Between the Impact and the Reliability of Evidence," *Organizational Behavior and Human Performance, 6* (1971), 111-131.

[100] Edgar M. Johnson, "The Effect of Data Source Reliability on Intuitive Inference," Technical Paper 251 (Arlington, VA: US Army Research Institute for the Behavioral and Social Sciences, 1974).

[101] R. R. Lau, M. R. Lepper, and L. Ross, "Persistence of Inaccurate and Discredited Personal Impressions: A Field Demonstration of Attributional Perseverance," paper presented at 56th Annual Meeting of the Western Psychological Association (Los Angeles, April 1976).

[102] Lee Ross, Mark R. Lepper, and Michael Hubbard, "Perseverance in Self-Perception and Social Perception: Biased Attributional Processes in the Debriefing Paradigm," *Journal of Personality and Social Psychology, 32*, 5, (1975), 880-892.

[103] Lee Ross, Mark R. Lepper, Fritz Strack, and Julia Steinmetz, "Social Explanation and Social Expectation: Effects of Real and Hypothetical Explanations on Subjective Likelihood," *Journal of Personality and Social Psychology, 33*, 11 (1977), 818.

[104] W. H. Walsh, *Philosophy of History: An Introduction* (Revised Edition: New York: Harper and Row, 1967), p. 61.

[105] Ellen J. Langer, "The Psychology of Chance," *Journal for the Theory of Social Behavior, 7* (1977), 185-208.

[106] Daniel Kahneman and Amos Tversky, "Subjective Probability: A Judgment of Representativeness," *Cognitive Psychology, 3* (1972), 430-54.

[107] W. Feller, *An Introduction to Probability Theory and Its Applications* (3rd Edition; New York: Wiley, 1968), p. 160.

[108] Gina Bari Kolata, "Paleobiology: Random Events over Geological Time," *Science*, 189 (1975), 625-626.

[109] Amos Tversky and Daniel Kahneman, "Belief in the Law of Small Numbers," *Psychological Bulletin*, 72, 2 (1971), 105-110.

[110] B. F. Skinner, "Superstition in the Pigeon," *Journal of Experimental Psychology*, 38 (1948), 168-172.

[111] Robert Jervis, *Perception and Misperception in International Politics* (Princeton, NJ: Princeton University Press, 1976), p. 320.

[112] For many historical examples, see Jervis, ibid., p. 321-23.

[113] Harold H. Kelley, "The Processes of Causal Attribution," *American Psychologist* (February 1973), p. 121.

[114] David Hackett Fischer, *Historian's Fallacies* (New York: Harper Torchbooks, 1970), p. 177.

[115] Ibid, p. 167.

[116] Richard E. Nisbett and Timothy DeC. Wilson, "Telling More Than We Can Know: Verbal Reports on Mental Processes," *Psychological Review* (May 1977), p. 252.

[117] Lee Ross, "The Intuitive Psychologist and his Shortcomings: Distortions in the Attribution Process," in Leonard Berkowitz, ed., *Advances in Experimental Social Psychology*, Volume 10 (New York: Academic Press, 1977), p. 184.

[118] Jervis, ibid., Chapter 2.

[119] Edward E. Jones, "How Do People Perceive the Causes of Behavior?" *American Scientist*, 64 (1976), p. 301.

[120] Daniel Heradstveit, *The Arab-Israeli Conflict: Psychological Obstacles to Peace* (Oslo: Universitetsforlaget, 1979), p. 25.

[121] See Richards J. Heuer, Jr., "Analyzing the Soviet Invasion of Afghanistan: Hypotheses from Causal Attribution Theory," *Studies in Comparative Communism*, Winter 1980. These comments concerning the Soviet invasion of Afghanistan are based solely on the results of psychological research, not on information concerning Soviet actions in Afghanistan or the US reaction thereto. The nature of generalizations concerning how people normally process information is that they apply "more or less" to many cases but may not offer a perfect fit to any single instance. There were obviously many other factors that influenced analysis of Soviet actions, including preconceptions concerning the driving forces behind Soviet policy. The intent is to illustrate the relevance of psychological research on the analytical process, not to debate the merits of alternative interpretations of Soviet policy. Thus I leave to the reader to judge how much his or her own interpretation of the Soviet invasion of Afghanistan may be influenced by these attributional tendencies.

[122] Edward Jones and Richard Nisbett, "The Actor and the Observer: Divergent Perceptions of Their Behavior," in Edward Jones *et al., Attribution: Perceiving the Causes of Behavior* (New Jersey: General Learning Press, 1971), p. 93.

[123] Based on personal discussion with CIA analysts.

[124] Raymond Tanter, "Bounded Rationality and Decision Aids," essay prepared for the Strategies of Conflict seminar, Mont Pelerin, Switzerland, 11-16 May 1980.

[125] This section draws heavily upon Jervis, Chapter 9.

[126] It follows from the same reasoning that we may underestimate the consequences of our actions on nations that are not the *intended* target of our influence.

[127] This paragraph draws heavily from the ideas and phraseology of Baruch Fischhoff, "For Those Condemned to Study the Past: Reflections on Historical Judgment," in R. A. Shweder and D. W. Fiske, eds., *New Directions for Methodology of Behavioral Science: Fallible Judgment in Behavioral Research* (San Francisco: Jossey-Bass, 1980).

[128] Jan Smedslund, "The Concept of Correlation in Adults," *Scandinavian Journal of Psychology*, Vol. 4 (1963), 165-73.

[129] Robert Axelrod, "The Rational Timing of Surprise," *World Politics*, XXXI (January 1979), pp. 228-246.

[130] Barton Whaley, *Stratagem: Deception and Surprise in War*, (Cambridge, MA: Massachusetts Institute of Technology, unpublished manuscript, 1969), p. 247.

[131] E. H. Carr, *What is History?* (London: Macmillan, 1961), p. 126, cited by Fischhoff, *op. cit.*

[132] Ross, *op. cit.*, pp. 208-209.

[133] Amos Tversky and Daniel Kahneman, "Availability: A Heuristic for Judging Frequency and Probability," *Cognitive Psychology*, 5 (1973), pp. 207-232.

[134] Ibid., p. 229.

[135] John S. Carroll, "The Effect of Imagining an Event on Expectations for the Event: An Interpretation in Terms of the Availability Heuristic", *Journal of Experimental Social Psychology*, 14 (1978), pp. 88-96.

[136] Amos Tversky and Daniel Kahneman, "Judgment under Uncertainty: Heuristics and Biases," *Science*, Vol. 185, Sept. 27, 1974, pp. 1124-1131.

[137] Experiments using a 98-percent confidence range found that the true value fell outside the estimated range 40 to 50 percent of the time. Amos Tversky and Daniel Kahneman, "Anchoring and Calibration in the Assessment of Uncertain Quantities," (Oregon Research Institute Research Bulletin, 1972, Nov. 12, No. 5), and M. Alpert and H. Raiffa, "A Progress Report on The Training of Probability Assessors," Unpublished manuscript, Harvard University, 1968.

[138] Alpert and Raiffa, ibid.

[139] Nicholas Schweitzer, "Bayesian Analysis: Estimating the Probability of Middle East Conflict," in Richards J. Heuer, Jr., ed., *Quantitative Approaches to Political Intelligence: The CIA Experience* (Boulder, CO: Westview Press, 1979). Jack Zlotnick, "Bayes' Theorem for Intelligence Analysis," *Studies in Intelligence*, Vol. 16, No. 2 (Spring 1972). Charles E. Fisk, "The Sino-Soviet Border Dispute: A Comparison of the Conventional and Bayesian Methods for Intelligence Warning", *Studies in Intelligence*, vol. 16, no. 2 (Spring 1972), originally classified Secret, now declassified. Both the Zlotnick and Fisk articles were republished in H. Bradford Westerfield, *Inside CIA's Private World: Declassified Articles from the Agency's Internal Journal, 1955-1992*, (New Haven: Yale University Press, 1995).

[140] For another interpretation of this phenomenon, see Chapter 13, "Hindsight Biases in Evaluation of Intelligence Reporting."

[141] Scott Barclay et al, *Handbook for Decision Analysis.* (McLean, VA: Decisions and Designs, Inc. 1977), p. 66.

[142] Sherman Kent, "Words of Estimated Probability," in Donald P. Steury, ed., *Sherman Kent and the Board of National Estimates: Collected Essays* (CIA, Center for the Study of Intelligence, 1994).

[143] Scott Barclay et al, p. 76-68.

[144] Probability ranges attributed to Kent in this table are slightly different from those in Sherman Kent, "Words of Estimated Probability," in Donald P. Steury, ed., *Sherman Kent and the Board of National Estimates: Collected Essays* (CIA, Center for the Study of Intelligence, 1994).

[145] Paul Slovic, Baruch Fischhoff, and Sarah Lichtenstein, "Cognitive Processes and Societal Risk Taking," in J. S. Carroll and J.W. Payne, eds., *Cognition and Social Behavior* (Potomac, MD: Lawrence Erlbaum Associates, 1976), pp. 177-78.

[146] This is a modified version, developed by Frank J. Stech, of the blue and green taxicab question used by Kahneman and Tversky, "On Prediction and Judgment," Oregon Research Institute Research Bulletin, 12, 14, 1972.

[147] Maya Bar-Hillel, "The Base-Rate Fallacy in Probability Judgments," *Acta Psychologica*, 1980.

[148] Many examples from everyday life are cited in Robyn M. Dawes, *Rational Choice in an Uncertain World* (Harcourt Brace Jovanovich College Publishers, 1988), Chapter 5.

[149] This chapter was first published as an unclassified article in *Studies in Intelligence*, Vol. 22, No. 2 (Summer 1978), under the title "Cognitive Biases: Problems in Hindsight Analysis." It was later published in H. Bradford Westerfield, editor, *Inside CIA's Private World: Declassified Articles from the Agency's Internal Journal, 1955-1992* (New Haven: Yale University Press, 1995.)

[150] This section is based on research reported by Baruch Fischoff and Ruth Beyth in "I Knew It Would Happen: Remembered Probabilities of Once-Future Things," *Organizational Behavior and Human Performance*, 13 (1975), pp. 1-16.

[151] Experiments described in this section are reported in Baruch Fischhoff, *The Perceived Informativeness of Factual Information*, Technical Report DDI- I (Eugene, OR: Oregon Research Institute, 1976).

[152] Experiments described in this section are reported in Baruch Fischhoff, "Hindsight does not equal Foresight: The Effect of Outcome Knowledge on Judgment Under Uncertainty," *Journal of Experimental Psychology: Human Perception and Performance*, 1, 3 (1975), pp. 288-299.

[153] Roberta Wohlstetter, *Pearl Harbor: Warning and Decision* (Stanford, CA: Stanford University Press, 1962), p. 387. Cited by Fischhoff.

[154] Roberta Wohlstetter, *Pearl Harbor: Warning and Decision* (Stanford: Stanford University Press, 1962), p. 302.

[155] Graham Allison's work on the Cuban missile crisis (Essence of Decision, Little, Brown & Co., 1971) is an example of what I have in mind. Allison identified three alternative assumptions about how governments work--the rational actor model, organizational process model, and bureaucratic politics model. He then showed how an analyst's implicit assumptions about the most appropriate model for analyzing a foreign government's behavior cause him or her to focus on different evidence and arrive at different conclusions. Another example is my own analysis of five alternative paths for making counterintelligence judgments in the controversial case of KGB defector Yuriy Nosenko. Richards J. Heuer, Jr., "Nosenko: Five Paths to Judgment," *Studies in Intelligence*, Vol. 31, No. 3 (Fall 1987), originally classified Secret but declassified and published in H. Bradford Westerfield, ed., *Inside CIA's Private World: Declassified Articles from the Agency Internal Journal 1955-1992* (New Haven: Yale University Press, 1995).

[156] Transcript of Adm. David Jeremiah's news conference at CIA, 2 June 1998.

INDEX

autonomy, 49
availability, 42, 128, 153, 154, 155, 164
averaging, 161
awareness, 5, 7, 21, 39, 117, 142, 144, 157, 186

B

bargaining, 139, 140, 182
base rate, 162, 164
base rates, 164
behavior, 9, 17, 49, 52, 53, 135, 139, 141, 142, 143, 144, 145, 146, 147, 193, 205
belief systems, 34
bias, 3, 4, 10, 28, 121, 122, 131, 137, 139, 141, 142, 143, 144, 145, 154, 157, 166, 167, 168, 169, 173, 174
blame, 145, 173, 186
blocks, 88
body, 25, 28, 61, 72, 75, 87, 121, 127, 131, 164
brain, vii, 32, 34, 79
brainstorming, 88, 180
breakfast, 37

C

cables, 73
campaigns, 53
cancer, 128, 154
candidates, 7, 145
capsule, 129
causal relationship, 98, 141, 144, 153, 162, 163
causality, 136, 142, 144
causation, 146
cell, 110, 112, 148, 150, 151
chain of command, 80, 180
changing environment, 43
channels, 8, 17, 78, 132
chicken, 37
children, 145

China, 17
CIA, v, vii, ix, xi, 1, 2, 3, 4, 5, 6, 7, 10, 123, 126, 143, 154, 155, 170, 173, 185, 191, 193, 198, 202, 203, 204, 205
cigarette smoking, 128
classes, 123
classroom, 16, 156, 185, 197
closure, 28
clustering, 138
cognitive biases, 121, 122, 166
cognitive map, 98
cognitive performance, 11
cognitive process, vii, 65, 133, 184
cognitive psychology, xi, 15, 17, 74, 105, 121
coherence, 136, 137
Cold War, 1, 143
collaboration, 4
commitment, ix, 8, 25, 84
communication, xi, 86, 91, 159
community, ix, 18
compatibility, 9
competition, 9, 84
complexity, 16, 23, 34, 40, 73, 95, 96, 121, 122, 136
components, 31, 109
comprehension, 38
concentrates, 60
concentration, 88
conception, 36
conceptual model, 53
concrete, 48, 51, 108, 125, 126, 127, 128, 129
conditioning, 54, 138
conduct, 28, 66, 67, 165, 183, 188
confidence, viii, ix, 26, 52, 65, 67, 68, 71, 72, 82, 129, 130, 131, 132, 156, 169, 203
configuration, 74
conflict, 23, 50, 91, 92
conformity, 186
confusion, 140, 141, 182
conscious awareness, 15

D

E

models, vii, 8, 9, 11, 17, 18, 19, 57, 69,
    73, 74, 75, 81, 184
monitoring, 15, 180, 189
mosaic, 74, 75
Moscow, 41, 167
motivation, 16, 92, 132
movement, 32, 41, 50
MRI, 34
multidimensional, 35, 78
multiple regression, 70
multiple regression analysis, 70
multiplication, 96

N

national interests, 82, 143
National Security Council, 3
nationalism, 143
NATO, 159
natural selection, 138
needs, ix, 35, 48, 61, 80, 86, 92, 115,
    128, 148, 180, 186
network, 35
neuron, 34
neurons, 34, 79
newspapers, 61, 125, 181
nodes, 35
noise, 77
novelty, 85
nuclear weapons, 82, 85, 117, 145, 187,
    188
nurses, 147

O

obesity, 152
objective criteria, 186
objectivity, 27, 56, 165, 173, 174, 175,
    186
observations, ix, 11, 17, 75, 125, 127,
    136, 137, 151
octopus, 34
Oklahoma, 196, 199

openness, 42, 78
organization, viii, 15, 19, 28, 31, 35, 40,
    56, 91, 136, 185
organizational behavior, 56
orientation, 144
outline, 106, 191
overload, ix
oxygen, 96

P

pain, 4
parents, 145
passive, 21
pathology, 48
pathways, 35
peer review, 8, 81
perceptions, 22, 24, 26, 27, 28, 36, 127,
    144, 151, 166, 170, 172, 174, 180
performers, 39
permit, 149
perseverance, 92, 134
personal qualities, 135, 142
personality, 17, 68, 133, 134, 141
personality traits, 133
perspective, 17, 25, 28, 35, 50, 57, 82,
    83, 84, 87, 88, 139, 143, 167, 169
physical properties, 140
planning, 111, 117, 139, 160, 164, 188
plausibility, 105, 155
political instability, 51
politics, 193, 205
polling, 53, 130
poor, 74, 99, 106, 118, 122, 133
population, 128, 130
positive reinforcement, 138
power, 6, 49, 51, 85, 187
predictability, 139
prediction, 67, 68, 70, 160, 168
predictive accuracy, 71
preference, 110, 144
prejudice, 122
pressure, 27, 62, 84, 117, 145

T